PUBLISHED BY
© SOFT SKULL PRESS
71 BOND ST.
BROOKLYN NY 11217
WWW.SOFTSKULL.COM

BOOK AND
COVER DESIGN BY
CHARLES ORR

PRINTED IN CANADA
DISTRIBUTED BY
PUBLISHERS GROUP WEST
1-800-788-3123
WWW.PGW.COM

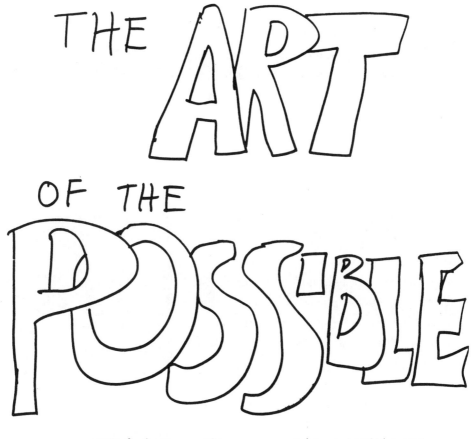

THE ART OF THE POSSIBLE

COMICS MAINLY WITHOUT PICTURES

BY KENNETH KOCH

INTRODUCTION BY DAVID LEHMAN

Kenneth Koch loved comics—comic books, comic strips, and cartoons—in their actual state and for their poetic potential. "I read them as sheep graze grass," he once said, and he found ways to translate his enjoyment into the writing of poetry. Hamlet may have had to put on an antic disposition. It came naturally to Kenneth. But letting comics into his literary imagination followed not only from his love of the humorous, the whimsical, and the witty, but from an aesthetic point of view that could be characterized as defiantly antiacademic. Koch liked T. S. Eliot's poetry but didn't see why an appreciation of "Prufrock" or "The Hollow Men" obliged him to follow the orthodox line of permitted enthusiasms laid down by Eliot and his devotees. A love of Eliot's poetry could coexist with a love of Popeye, Nancy, Mickey Mouse, or Marvel action heroes—the two didn't stand in contradiction. This notion has gradually gained acceptance and may not seem remarkable today, but it was revolutionary in the late 1940s and 1950s when Kenneth espoused it as a young poet in New York.

KENYA COMICS
LATE THAT NIGHT
WHEN THE ELE-PHANTS
WERE ASLEEP
THEY ALL HAD
AGITATED DREAMS
THEY DREAMED THEY WERE SWEARING
TO TELL THE TRUTH
AGAIN
AND AGAIN

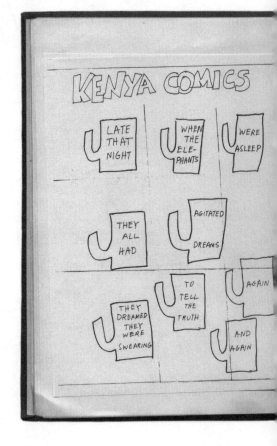

Kenneth came of age during the heyday of the New Criticism when a poem had to meet the criteria of the "well-wrought urn": taut webs of ambiguity, difficulty, and complexity earned the highest hosannas. Like his Harvard friend John Ashbery, who went on to write a sestina about Popeye and a comic pastoral called "Daffy Duck in Hollywood," Kenneth felt that the canon of modern American poetry desperately needed to be broadened and that it was just as legitimate to turn to comic books as to French and Italian poetry, or to modern painting, for inspiration.

What Kenneth found particularly inspiring in comics was their exclamatory American freshness and exuberance and their capacity for joy. These are virtues of his own poetry. Early on he found he could transmute anger and outrage into a pleasure-giving poem that masked its threatening nature. In "Fresh Air" (1955), his tirade against university hacks and stuffed shirts, the action figure known as "the Strangler" turns up in the nick of time to "annihilate the students of myth" and terminate the purveyors of what Koch elsewhere calls "'kiss-me-I'm-poetical' junk":

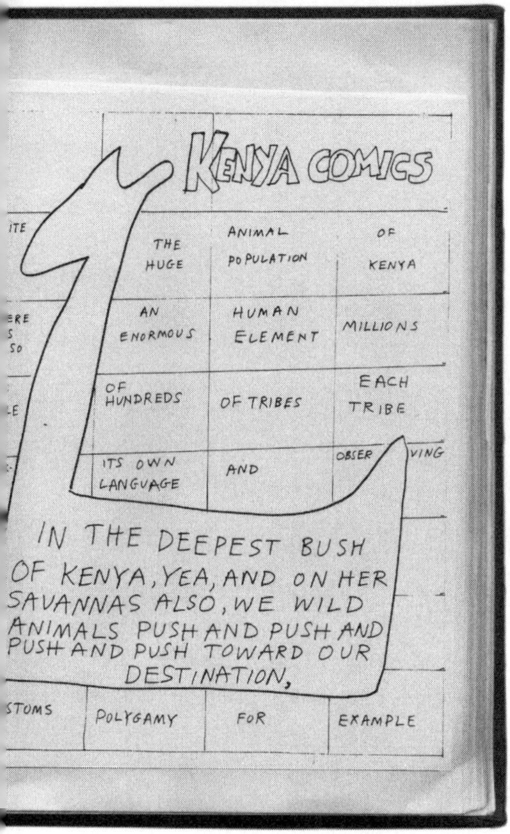

> Here on the railroad train, one more time, is
>   the Strangler.
> He is going to get that one there, who is
>   on his way to a poetry reading.
> Agh! Biff! A body falls to the moving floor.
>
> In the football stadium I also see him,
> He leaps through the frosty air at the
>   maker of comparisons
> Between football and life and silently, silently
>   strangles him!

There is an animating tension between the comic book language ("Agh! Biff!") and action ("leaps through the frosty air"), on the one side, and the poem's ferocious aggression on the other. The humor doesn't undercut the anger. It makes it more potent.

For Kenneth it was an article of faith that the comic no less than the solemn, the comic book no less than the Elizabethan sonnet or the Romantic ode, has its place in the world of seriousness and can provide the fodder or the structure, the spirit or the form of a poem. The comic book panel was like the line in poetry, a unit of composition, suggesting "new ways of talking about things and dividing

KENYA COMICS

	THE HUGE	ANIMAL POPULATION	OF KENYA
	AN ENORMOUS	HUMAN ELEMENT	MILLIONS
	OF HUNDREDS	OF TRIBES	EACH TRIBE
	ITS OWN LANGUAGE	AND	OBSERVING
	POLYGAMY	FOR	EXAMPLE

IN THE DEEPEST BUSH OF KENYA, YEA, AND ON HER SAVANNAS ALSO, WE WILD ANIMALS PUSH AND PUSH AND PUSH AND PUSH TOWARD OUR DESTINATION,

KOCH'S ORIGINAL MOCKED-UP BOOK PROPOSAL.

them up." Take section four of "The Circus" and see if it doesn't lend strength to the comparison:

Minnie the Rabbit fingered her machine gun.
The bright day was golden.
She aimed the immense pine needle at the
  foxes
Thinking Now they will never hurt my tribe
  any more.

Or consider "The Interpretation of Dreams," in which Snow White is rescued from "Walt Disney's fiction" and given room to roam:

Meanwhile Snow White and her boyfriend
Have gone up into the mountains.
It is amazing what they will do for a game of
  bingo!
No! That is not what they are doing. Look!
They are making love! I didn't know that was
  allowed in the movies
In this country! But that must be what they are
  doing!

AUTOBIOGRAPHY
COMICS
to Janice
1955
DOWNSTAIRS
IN OUR BUILDING
LIVED
FERNAND LEGER
LA (THE) COURTYARD
LA GRANDE PORTE THE FRONT DOOR
La rue du Cherche-Midi

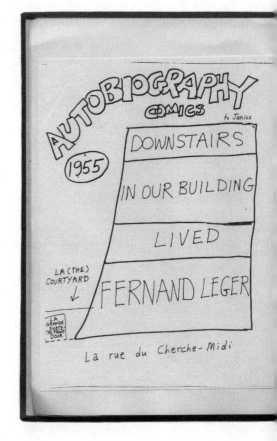

As a kid Kenneth had wanted to be a cartoonist before discovering poetry in a volume of Shelley (pictured on the cover with open-collared shirt and wild hair) that his uncle had kept in a safe. As a grown-up Kenneth saw no need to outgrow or renounce the comic books of childhood. He admired their naiveté, their lack of air and pretense. In conversation with David Shapiro, he remarked that he "liked the real emotional tug people had toward Mickey Mouse" and added that one rarely cared "as much about Hecuba as about Olive Oyl." Comics appealed to kids—why shouldn't poems? Why restrict poetry's constituency to "the dumb, the deaf, and the creepy"? Didn't some poems operate on principles similar to those of the comic book? Koch told Jordan Davis that both he and Ashbery read Spenser's *Faerie Queene* a year or two after graduating from Harvard. "When I asked him how he was liking it, he said it was wonderful, like reading an endless comic strip," Koch recalled.

Comics involved an exchange or interplay between words and pictures. It was like a collaboration between two media, and no poet valued artistic collaboration more highly than Kenneth, who collaborated with Ashbery on poems, with Joe Brainard on comic strips, and with Larry Rivers, Nell Blaine, Alex Katz, Red Grooms, and others on work in multiple media. Karen Koch informs me that Kenneth and legendary comic-book editor Stan Lee once planned a collaboration. This was during the late 1960s when the war in Vietnam was raging. Both Koch and Stan Lee adamantly opposed the war, and they came up with the idea of a "peace comic" that Koch would write and Lee would assign to an illustrator. What came of the project? "I can't quite recall why it never got much further," Ron Padgett says, "though I seem to remember Kenneth's telling me that eventually someone on Stan Lee's end found Kenneth's ideas or first draft to be too 'far out.'"

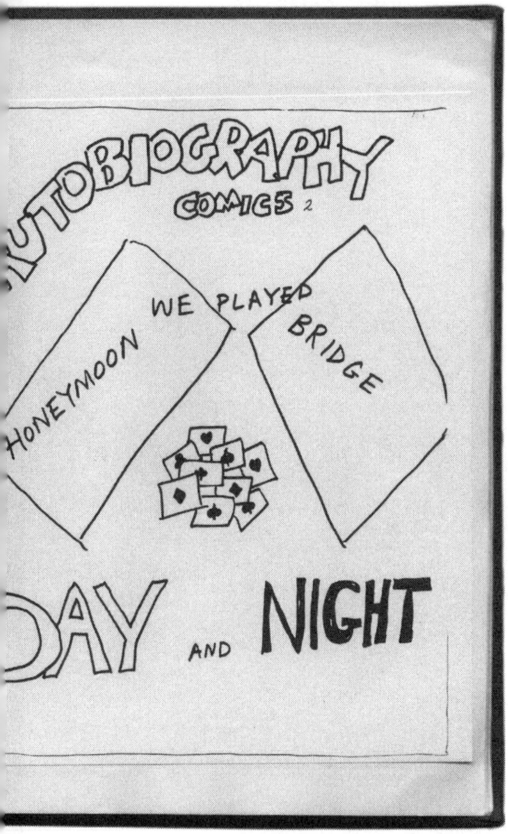

UTOBIOGRAPHY
COMICS 2
WE PLAYED
HONEYMOON
BRIDGE
DAY
AND
NIGHT

In Kenneth's famous course in imaginative writing at Columbia, one "far out" assignment was to buy a comic book (any genre), paste white paper over the balloons, and fill in your own dialogue. (You were—and this is crucial to the assignment—forbidden from reading the comic book first.) It was a great lesson in poetry as interpretation and mistranslation, for any succession of images can yield countless textual alternatives. Kenneth himself demonstrated this multiplicity in *Interlocking Lives* (Kulchur Press, 1970), the book that resulted from his collaboration with the painter Alex Katz. Katz produced the pictures, and Koch scrambled the order five different ways and wrote a narrative to go with each.

Kenneth was a great storyteller in poetry, and a singular aspect of his narrative poems is their capaciousness, the way they jump around from one plot to another. In Koch's poems, simultaneity has replaced hierarchy as a structural principle—a crucial word for Kenneth is *meanwhile*—and the subject matter can come equally from different time zones. All of experience and all of culture broadly defined are valid. Yes, poetry offers the pleasures of verbal and formal sophistication, the mastery of blank verse or ottava rima. And yes, a poem in its range of reference can include Leonardo's *Last Supper* and Paolo Uccello's magnificent red horses. But poetry can also make room for Zoo Man, Daredevil, Julian and Maddalo, and John L. Lewis, not to mention Beowulf, Robert E. Lee, Sir Barbarossa, and Baron Jeep—the historical, the fictive, the fantastical, and the unreal—thrown together as they are in the poem "The Pleasures of Peace" (1968) where you will also find sneak appearances by Fidel Castro, Robert Herrick, Delmore Schwartz, "men named Stuart" (Kenneth's father's name), and "the Hairdresser of Night."

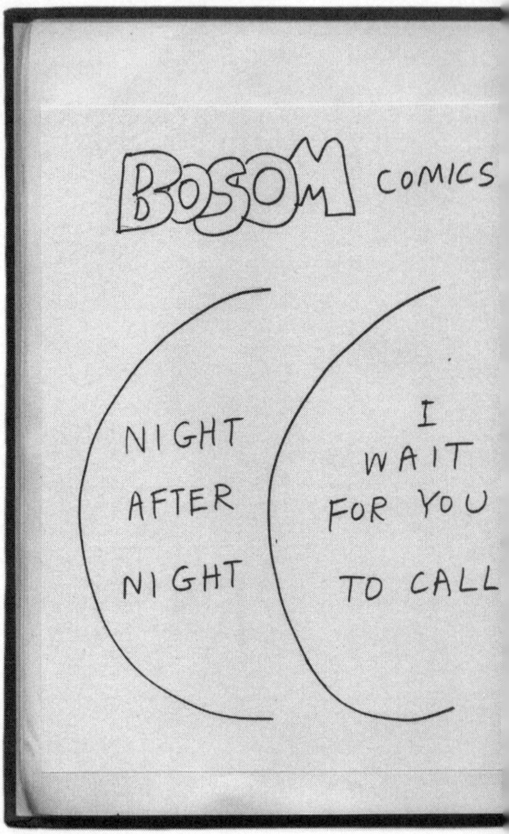
BOSOM COMICS
NIGHT AFTER NIGHT
I WAIT FOR YOU TO CALL

"The Pleasures of Peace" seems to me one of Kenneth's great achievements, succeeding as few poems of that period did in answering the call for a poem protesting the Vietnam War. In "The Pleasures of Peace," Koch characteristically turns a negative into a positive, writing not an antiwar poem in the approved manner ("To my contemporaries I'll leave the Horrors of War, / They can do them better than I") but a pro-peace celebration of poetry, Eros, the peace movement, the pleasure principle, and the poet's unconscious, all rolled into a ball: "It is the Night of the Painted Pajamas / And the Liberals are weeping for peace. The conservatives are raging for it. / The Independents are staging a parade. And we are completely naked / Walking through the bedroom for peace."

In 1992, Kenneth decided that not only could he borrow subject matter or adapt a narrative technique from comics but it might be possible to write poetry in a new form based on them. *The Art of the Possible* is the fruit of that decision. It is as high-spirited as Koch's fans would expect and extraordinarily inventive in treating the comic strip as a conceptual form "mainly without pictures." Koch's comics can work like the calligrammes of Apollinaire (consider "Bosom Comics") or like a box chart ("Different Kinds of Guys"). As happened earlier when he wrote *One Thousand Avant-Garde Plays* (Knopf, 1988), once the idea took hold with Kenneth, he went to town with it, creating sequences and subsequences: "Kenya Comics," "Autobiography Comics," "Hotel Igura Comics." These works are enchanting, smart, funny, and, in Duke Ellington's phrase, beyond category. My own favorite is "The Dead White Man" sequence with its corrosive wit reminiscent of "Fresh Air." The eponymous hero gets the last word: "If but one person reads me, then I am not really dead!!!"

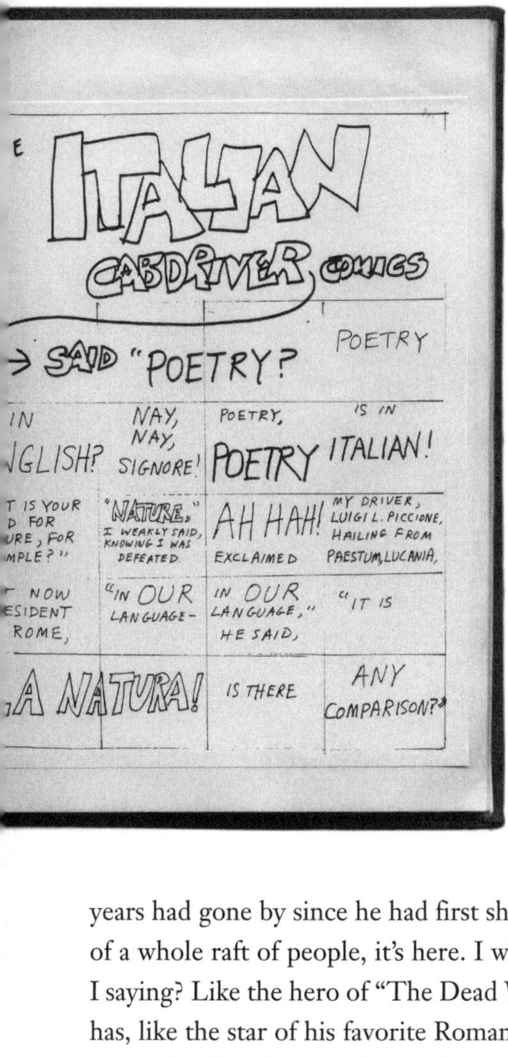

ITALIAN
CABDRIVER COMICS
SAID "POETRY?
POETRY
NAY, NAY, SIGNORE!
POETRY,
POETRY
IS IN
ITALIAN!
"NATURE,"
I WEAKLY SAID, KNOWING I WAS DEFEATED
AH HAH!
EXCLAIMED
MY DRIVER, LUIGI L. PICCIONE, HAILING FROM PAESTUM, LUCANIA,
"IN OUR LANGUAGE-
IN OUR LANGUAGE," HE SAID,
"IT IS
IS THERE
ANY COMPARISON?"

When I visited Kenneth six weeks before he died in July 2002, he made a point of saying how close to his heart was his poetry comic book still unpublished though nine years had gone by since he had first shown me the manuscript. Now thanks to the efforts of a whole raft of people, it's here. I wish Kenneth were around to enjoy it. But what am I saying? Like the hero of "The Dead White Man," Kenneth is not really dead. Rather he has, like the star of his favorite Romantic poet's elegy for Keats, outsoared the shadow of our night. You, dear reader, are keeping him alive.

THE ART OF THE POSSIBLE

CREDO:

VANISHING IS IMPOSSIBLE

LASTING IS IMPOSSIBLE

BEING IN TWO PLACES AT ONCE
IS IMPOSSIBLE

SPEAKING THE ENTIRE TRUTH
IS IMPOSSIBLE

INSTANTLY KNOWING SPANISH IS IMPOSSIBLE

LIVING IN THE MIDST OF TEN THOUSAND
PANES OF GLASS IS IMPOSSIBLE

BEING SIMULTANEOUSLY MASKED
AND UNMASKED IS IMPOSSIBLE

EXCEPT IN ART

ART IS THE ART OF THE POSSIBLE

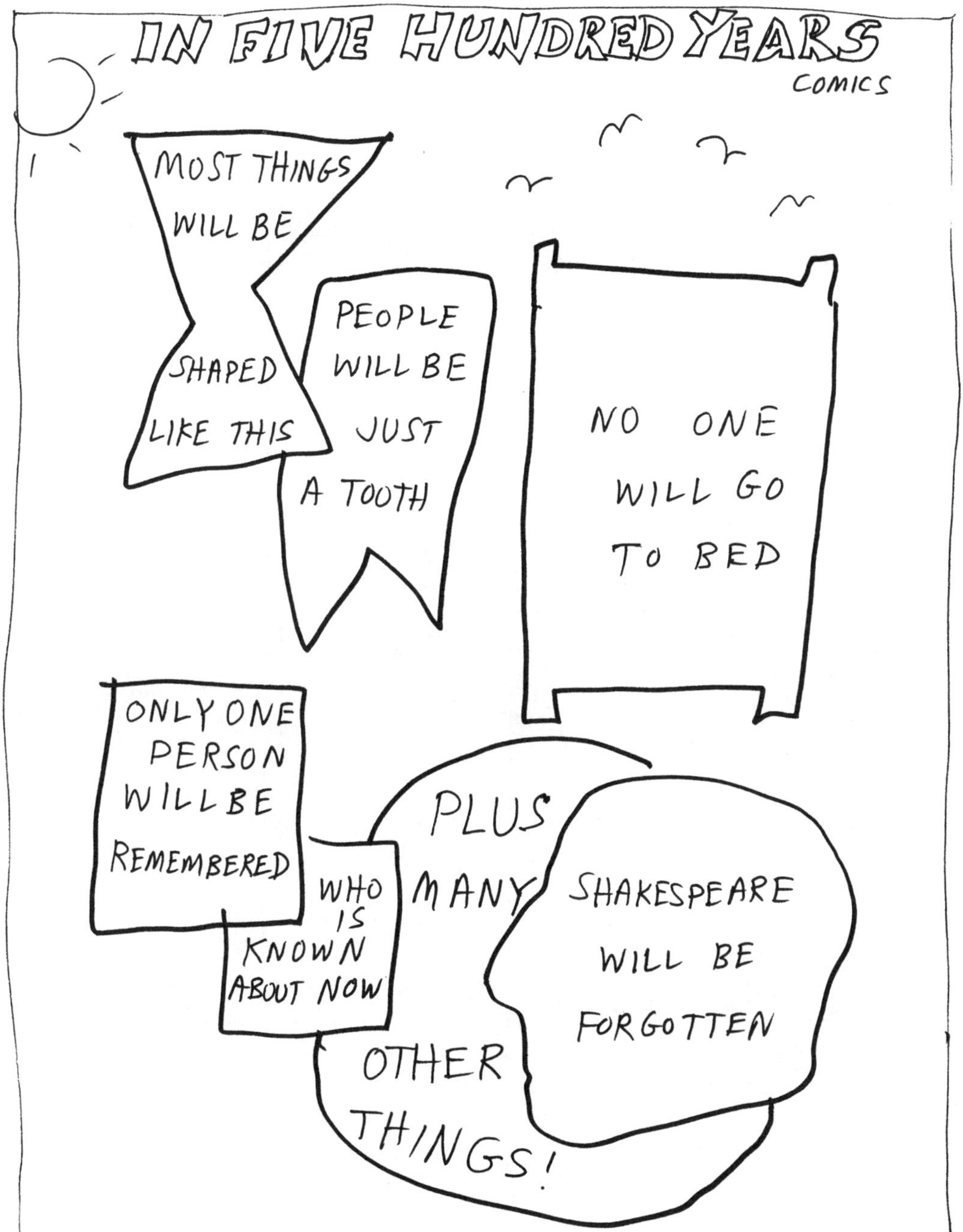
IN FIVE HUNDRED YEARS
COMICS
MOST THINGS WILL BE SHAPED LIKE THIS
PEOPLE WILL BE JUST A TOOTH
NO ONE WILL GO TO BED
ONLY ONE PERSON WILL BE REMEMBERED
WHO IS KNOWN ABOUT NOW
PLUS MANY OTHER THINGS!
SHAKESPEARE WILL BE FORGOTTEN

DIFFERENT KINDS OF GUYS

OK GUY	GOOD GUY	GREAT GUY	VOTIVE GUY
O.K. GUY BULLSHITS	GOOD GUY COMES ON OVER	GREAT GUY PASSES IN THE STREET	VOTIVE GUY IS POSED NEXT TO THE URN
"YEAH, O.K.!"	"SIT YE DOWN!"	LOVE LEANS OUT OF WINDOWS	ON THE HIGH ALTAR
HE GETS UP	"I'VE BROUGHT THE BABY."	HORROR KEEPS WITHIN	VOTIVE GUY IS LIGHTED IN HIS TWO CANDLES
HIS NOSE BLEEDS	"GIVE IT HERE!"	GREAT GUY GOES BY	VOTIVE GUY WAITS WHILE THE CANDLES BURN

DIFFERENT KINDS OF GALS

OK GAL	GOOD GAL	GREAT GAL	OLD GAL
FEELS SLEEPY	REMEMBERS BIRTHDAYS	READS MUSIC	EATS WHEAT BRAN
ROAMS ABOUT	WANTS TO TRAVEL	AND SINGS MADRIGALS	OFTEN DOZES
HER OLD APARTMENT	LIKES SLEEPING	AND GIVES THE MONEY	REMEMBERS TIMES
HOPES FOR MAIL	WITH A GREAT GUY	SHE EARNS TO THE NEEDY AND POOR	HAS A PIERCING GAZE

DIFFERENT KINDS OF HEMISPHERES

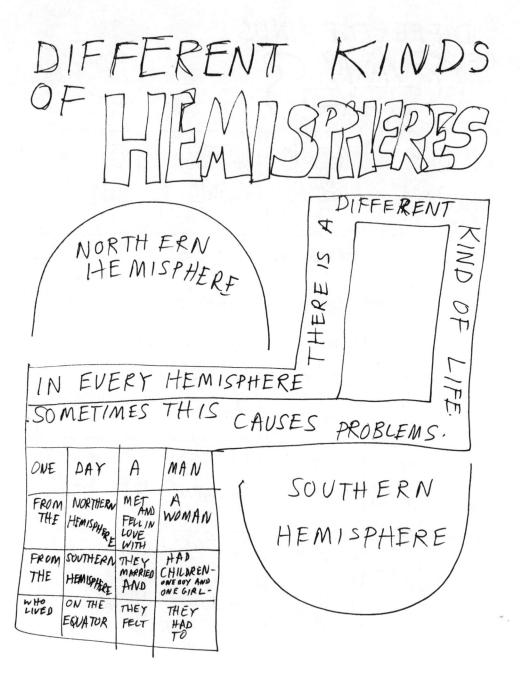

NORTHERN HEMISPHERE

THERE IS A DIFFERENT KIND OF LIFE

IN EVERY HEMISPHERE

SOMETIMES THIS CAUSES PROBLEMS.

SOUTHERN HEMISPHERE

ONE	DAY	A	MAN
FROM THE	NORTHERN HEMISPHERE	MET AND FELL IN LOVE WITH	A WOMAN
FROM THE	SOUTHERN HEMISPHERE	THEY MARRIED AND	HAD CHILDREN— ONE BOY AND ONE GIRL—
WHO LIVED	ON THE EQUATOR	THEY FELT	THEY HAD TO

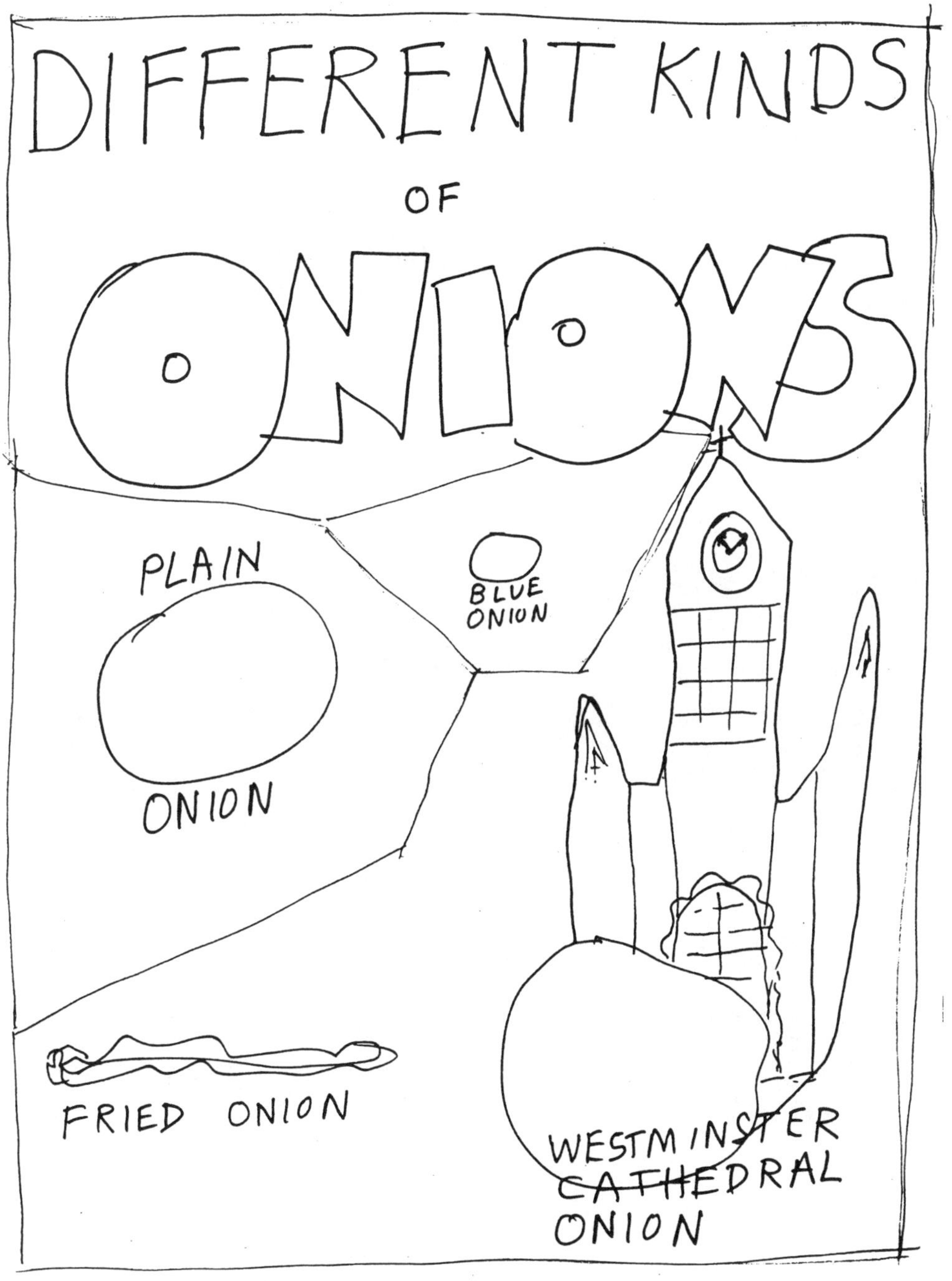
DIFFERENT KINDS
OF
ONIONS
PLAIN
ONION
BLUE
ONION
FRIED ONION
WESTMINSTER
CATHEDRAL
ONION

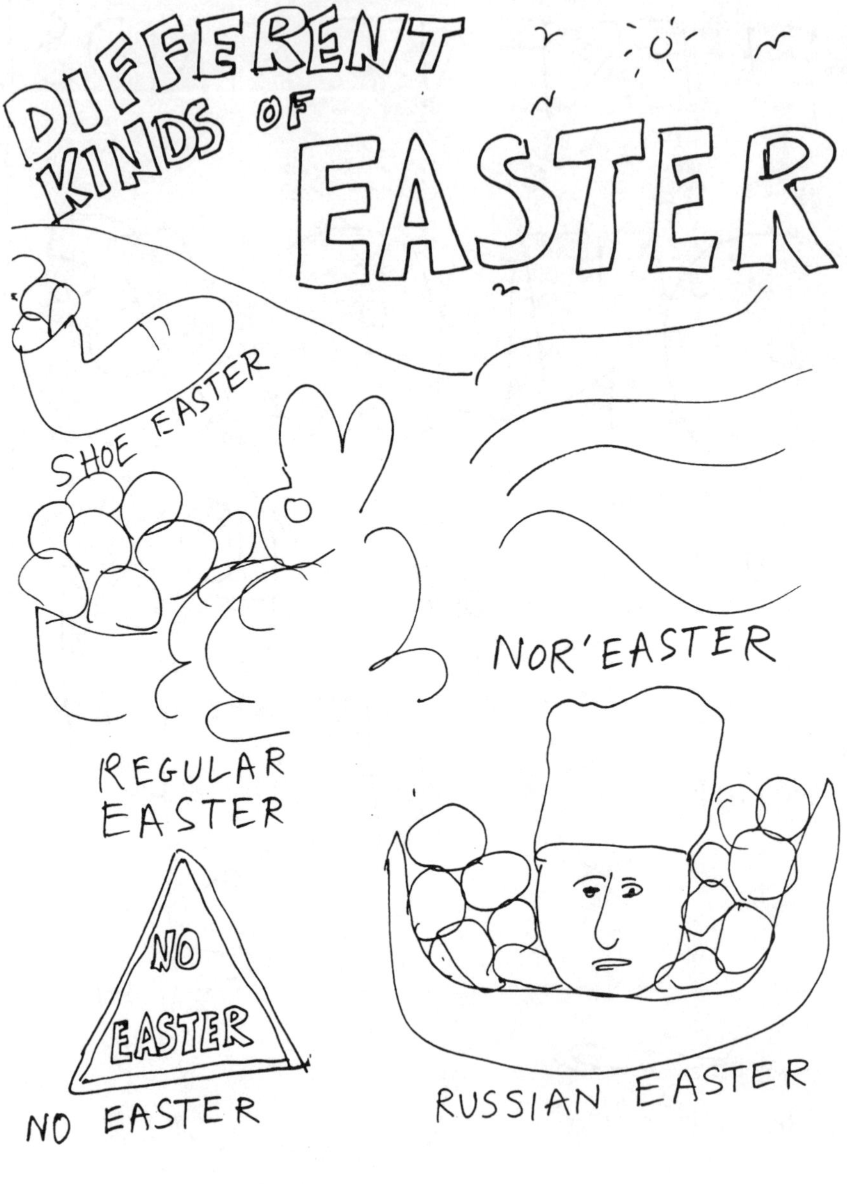
DIFFERENT KINDS OF EASTER
SHOE EASTER
REGULAR EASTER
NOR'EASTER
NO EASTER
EASTER
NO EASTER
RUSSIAN EASTER

DIFFERENT KINDS OF LIFE

MARINE LIFE

ANIMAL LIFE

HUMAN LIFE

THE AFTER LIFE

ANNUALS VS. PERENNIALS
FIRST KISS
VS.
JULY 4TH
HEAD ACHE
VS.
CELLS
MOUSE
VS.
MICE
CALLAS SINGS NORMA
VS.
EGYPT

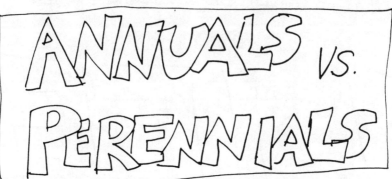

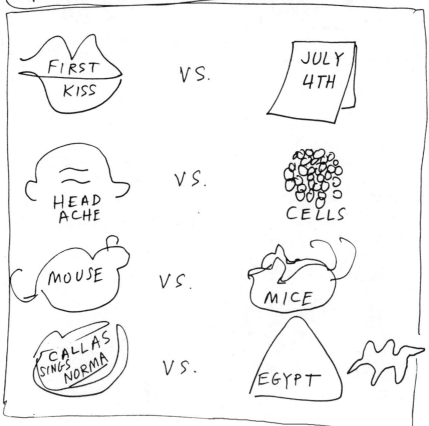

COMICS MYSTERY GAME

TOMB	"SECRET WOMAN"	FIRE ESCAPE
LETTER BOX	NOTE PAD	HOCKEY PLAYER
VILLAGE GREEN	INKSPOT	GAS PUMP
CLOCK	MANNEQUIN	TIGER

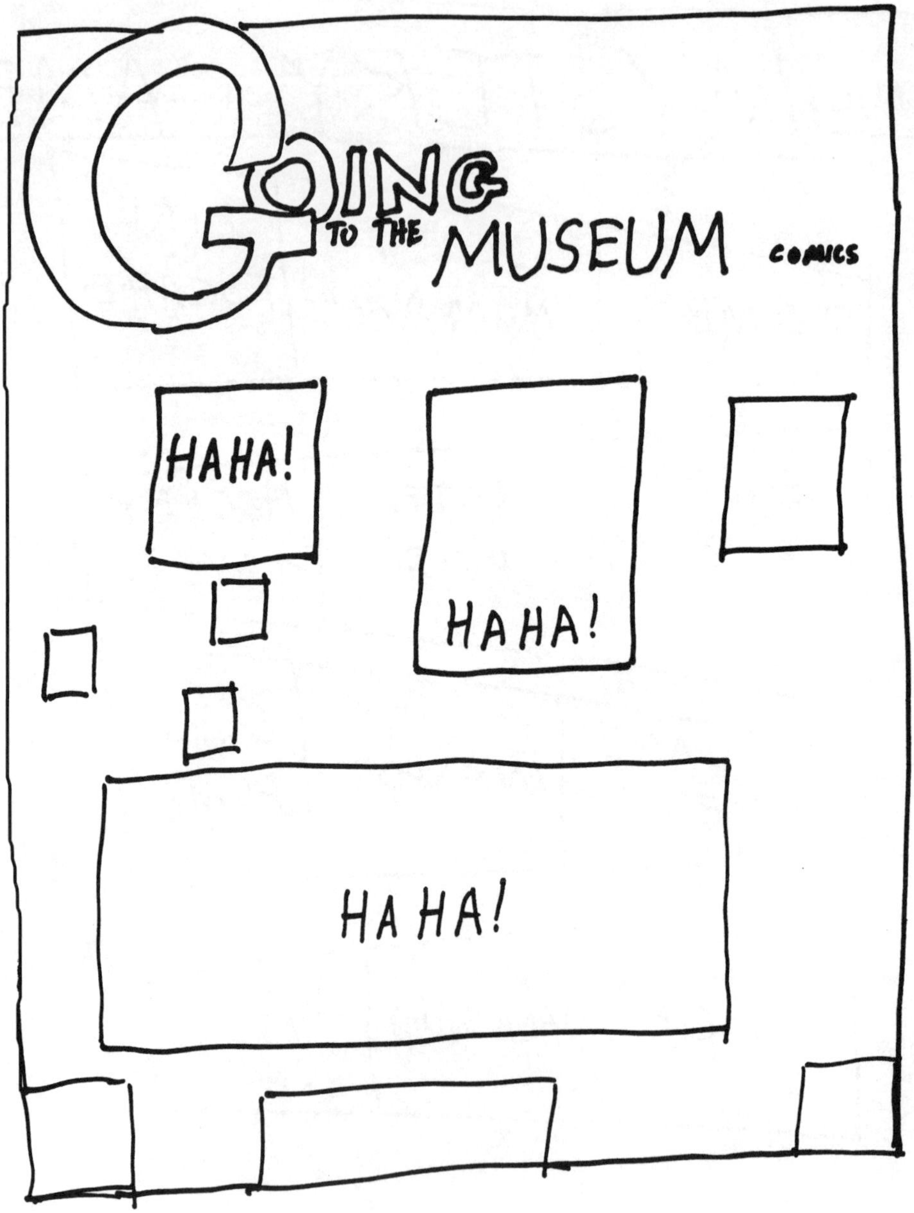
GOING TO THE MUSEUM COMICS
HAHA!
HAHA!
HAHA!

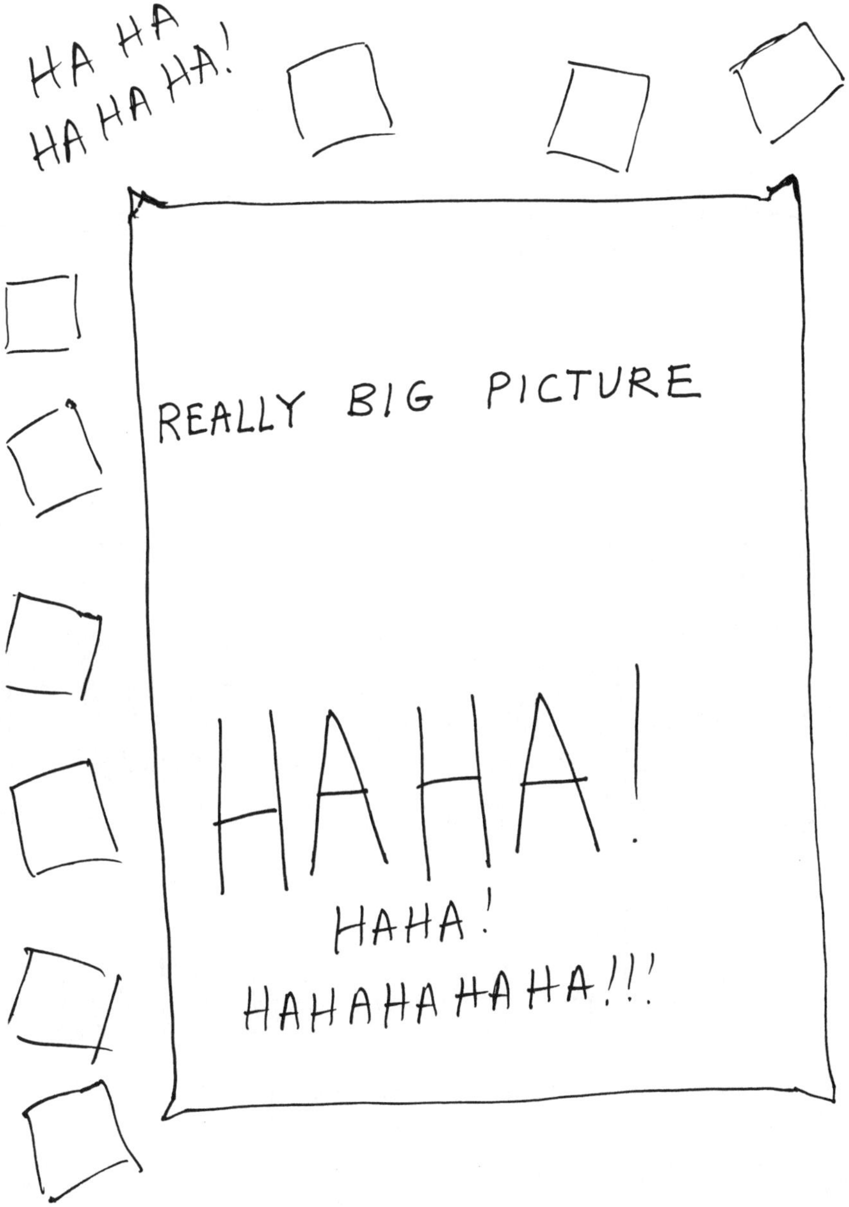
HA HA
HA HA HA HA!
REALLY BIG PICTURE
HAHA!
HAHA!
HAHAHAHAHAHA!!!

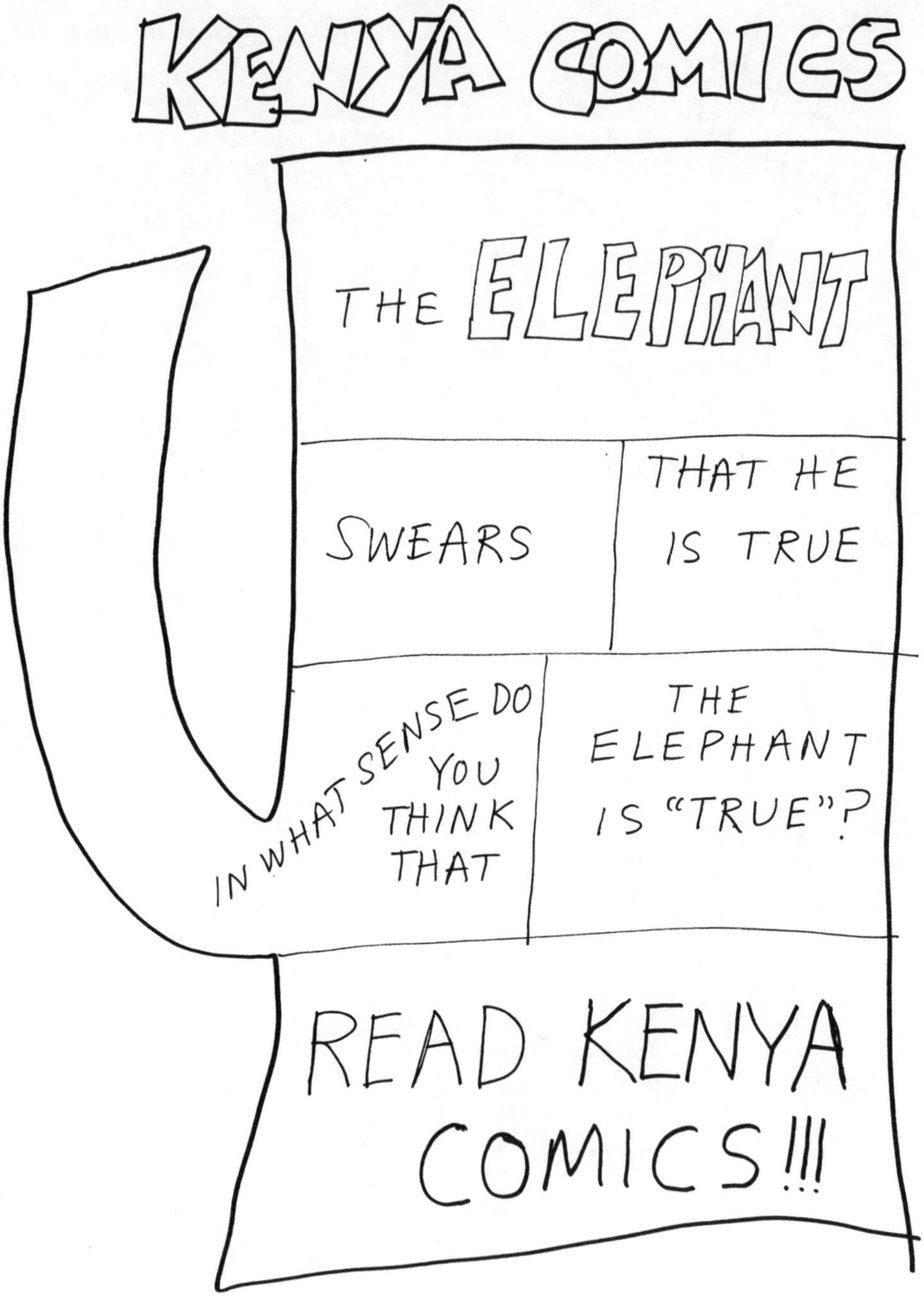
KENYA COMICS
THE ELEPHANT
SWEARS
THAT HE IS TRUE
IN WHAT SENSE DO YOU THINK THAT
THE ELEPHANT IS "TRUE"?
READ KENYA COMICS!!!

KENYA COMICS

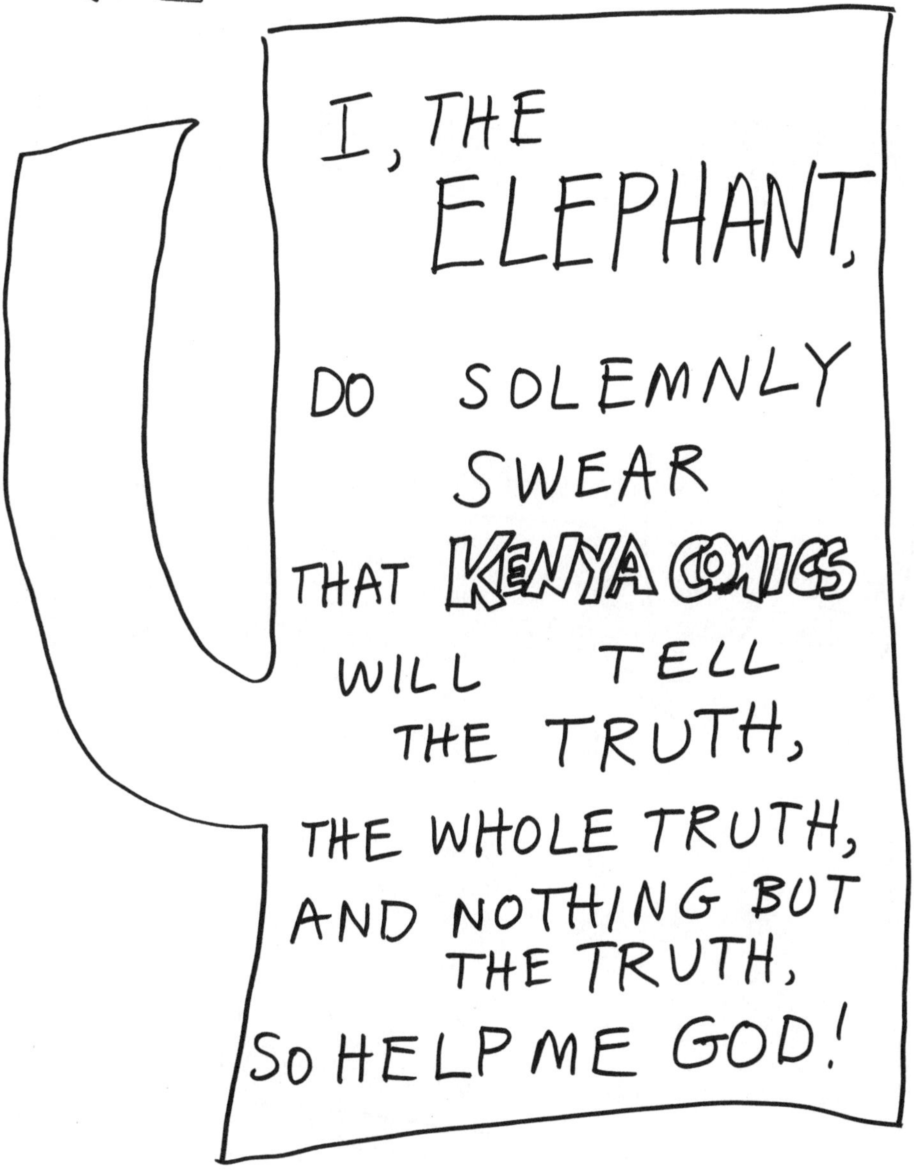
I, THE
ELEPHANT,
DO SOLEMNLY
SWEAR
THAT KENYA COMICS
WILL TELL
THE TRUTH,
THE WHOLE TRUTH,
AND NOTHING BUT
THE TRUTH,
SO HELP ME GOD!

KENYA COMICS

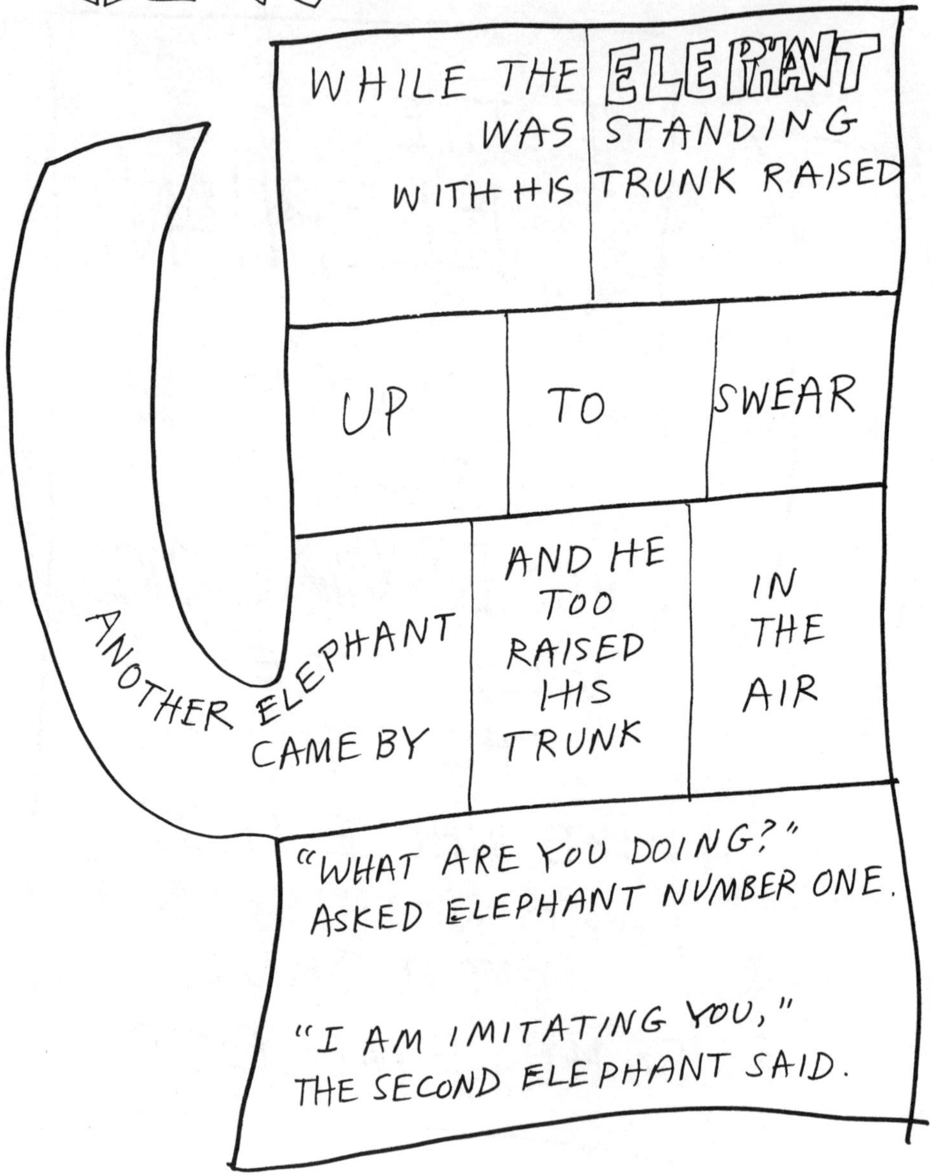
WHILE THE ELEPHANT
WAS STANDING
WITH HIS TRUNK RAISED
UP
TO
SWEAR
ANOTHER ELEPHANT CAME BY
AND HE TOO RAISED HIS TRUNK
IN THE AIR
"WHAT ARE YOU DOING?" ASKED ELEPHANT NUMBER ONE.
"I AM IMITATING YOU," THE SECOND ELEPHANT SAID.

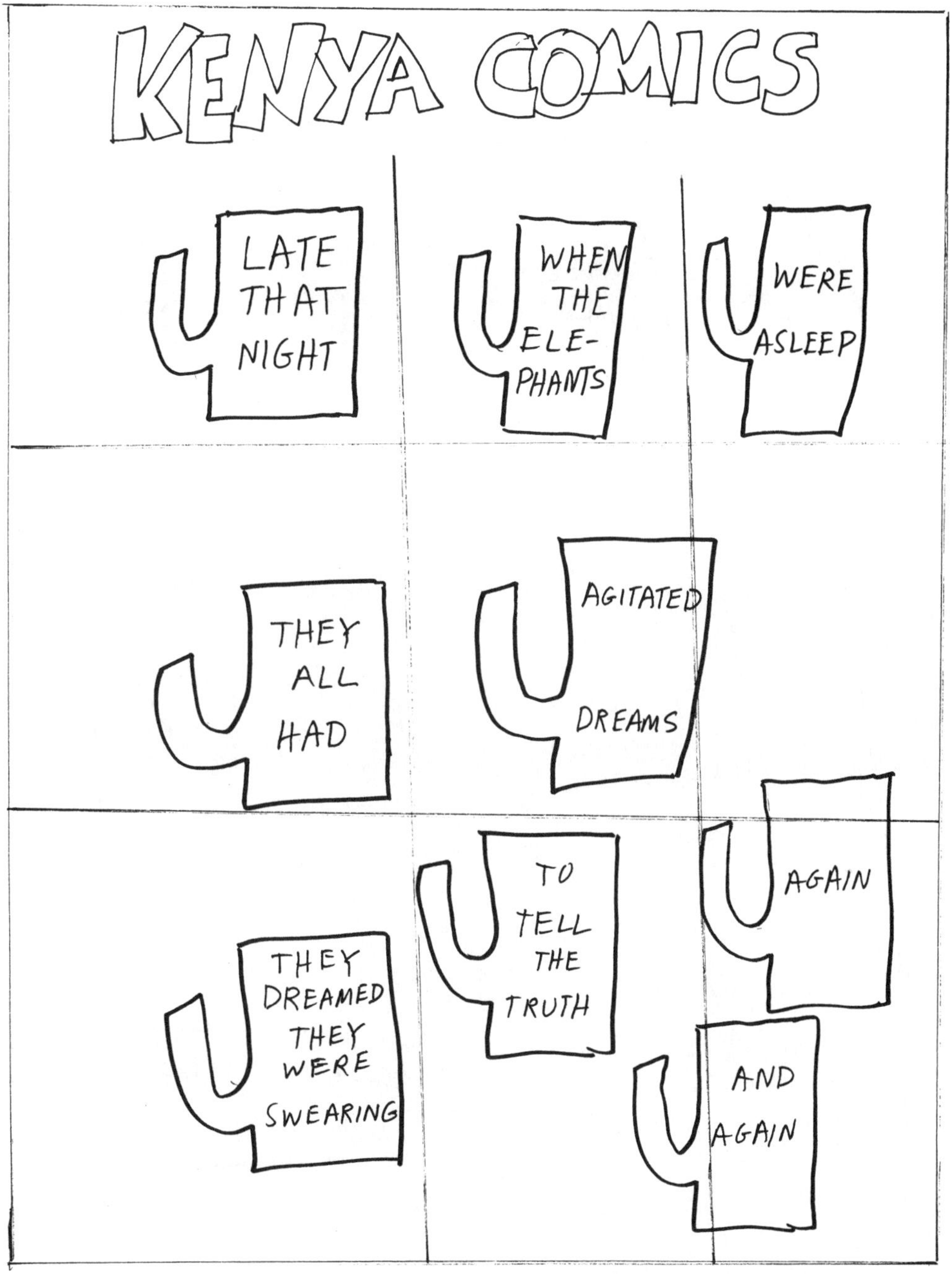
KENYA COMICS
LATE THAT NIGHT
WHEN THE ELE- PHANTS
WERE ASLEEP
THEY ALL HAD
AGITATED
DREAMS
THEY DREAMED THEY WERE SWEARING
TO TELL THE TRUTH
AGAIN
AND AGAIN

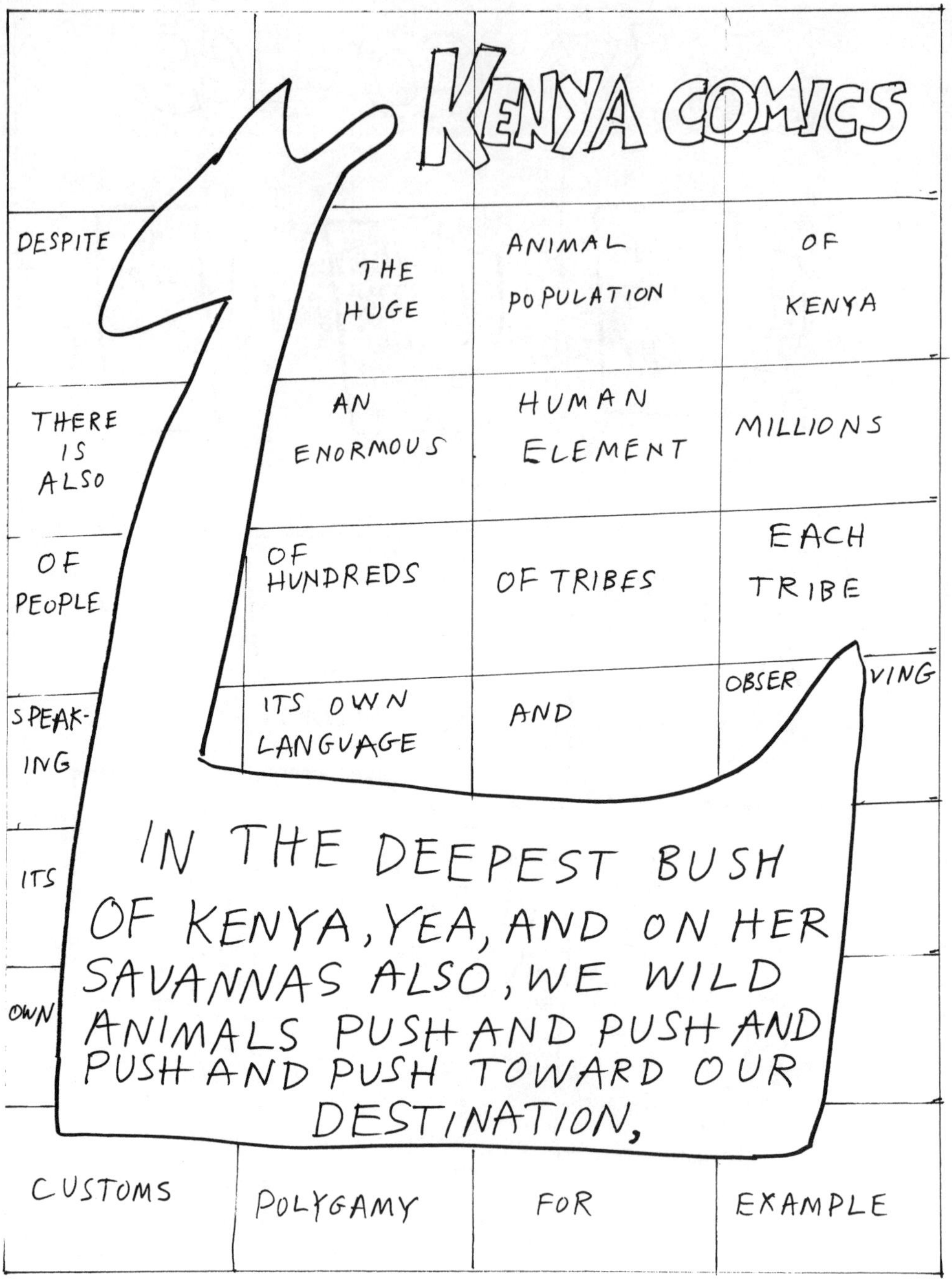

KENYA COMICS

DESPITE	THE HUGE	ANIMAL POPULATION	OF KENYA
THERE IS ALSO	AN ENORMOUS	HUMAN ELEMENT	MILLIONS
OF PEOPLE	OF HUNDREDS	OF TRIBES	EACH TRIBE
SPEAK-ING	ITS OWN LANGUAGE	AND	OBSERVING
ITS			
OWN			
CUSTOMS	POLYGAMY	FOR	EXAMPLE

IN THE DEEPEST BUSH OF KENYA, YEA, AND ON HER SAVANNAS ALSO, WE WILD ANIMALS PUSH AND PUSH AND PUSH AND PUSH TOWARD OUR DESTINATION,

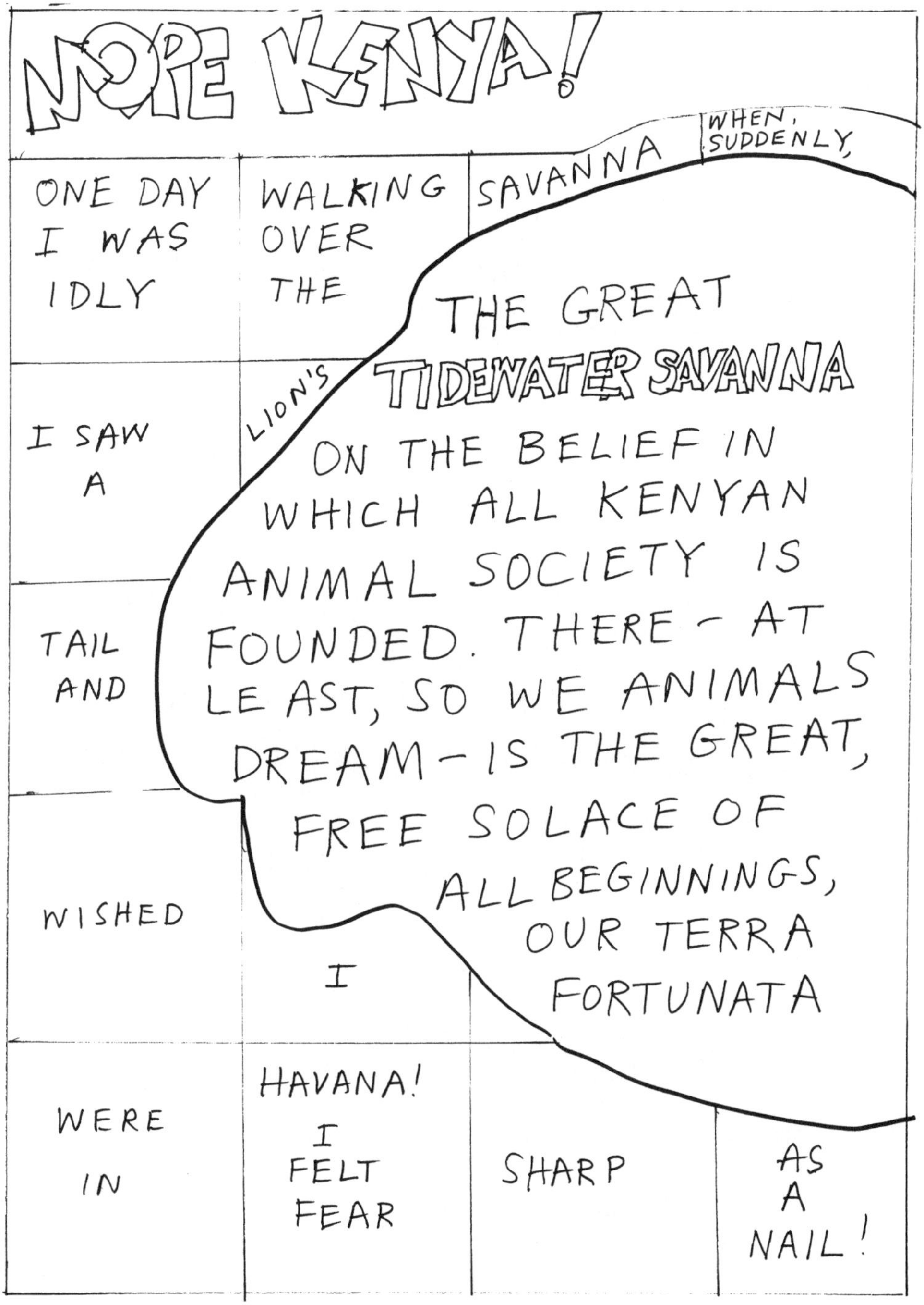

NOPE KENYA!

ONE DAY I WAS IDLY	WALKING OVER THE	SAVANNA	WHEN, SUDDENLY,
I SAW A	LION'S	THE GREAT TIDEWATER SAVANNA ON THE BELIEF IN WHICH ALL KENYAN ANIMAL SOCIETY IS FOUNDED. THERE — AT LEAST, SO WE ANIMALS DREAM — IS THE GREAT, FREE SOLACE OF ALL BEGINNINGS, OUR TERRA FORTUNATA	
TAIL AND			
WISHED	I		
WERE IN	HAVANA! I FELT FEAR	SHARP	AS A NAIL!

KENYA!

THIS TERRA FORTUNATA IS KNOWN TO US FROM DOCUMENTS AND TREATIES OF OLD, THAT STATE: "IN THE BODY OF EACH FEMALE AND MALE IS DEPOSITED THAT COMMON, SIMPLE WISDOM WHICH, GIVEN THE RIGHT CONDITIONS–RESIDENCE IN THE TERRA FORTUNATA–IS A GUARANTEE OF HAPPINESS."

THE UNION THROWS ITS PLAN OPEN TO THE MEMBERSHIP LET IT

DECIDE ON

WATER WAVE LENGTHS

HOLES AND

NOW AND TILL

THE SUCH

END OF

TIME AS IS ENVISAGED FEEBLY

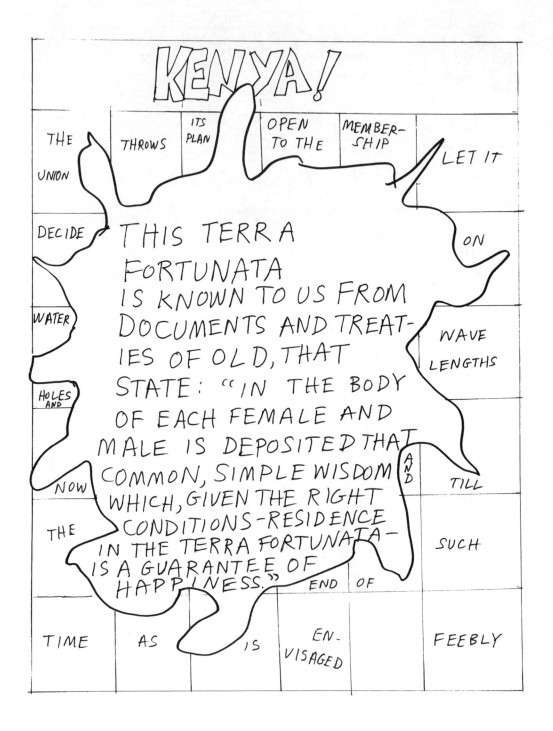

KENYA COMICS

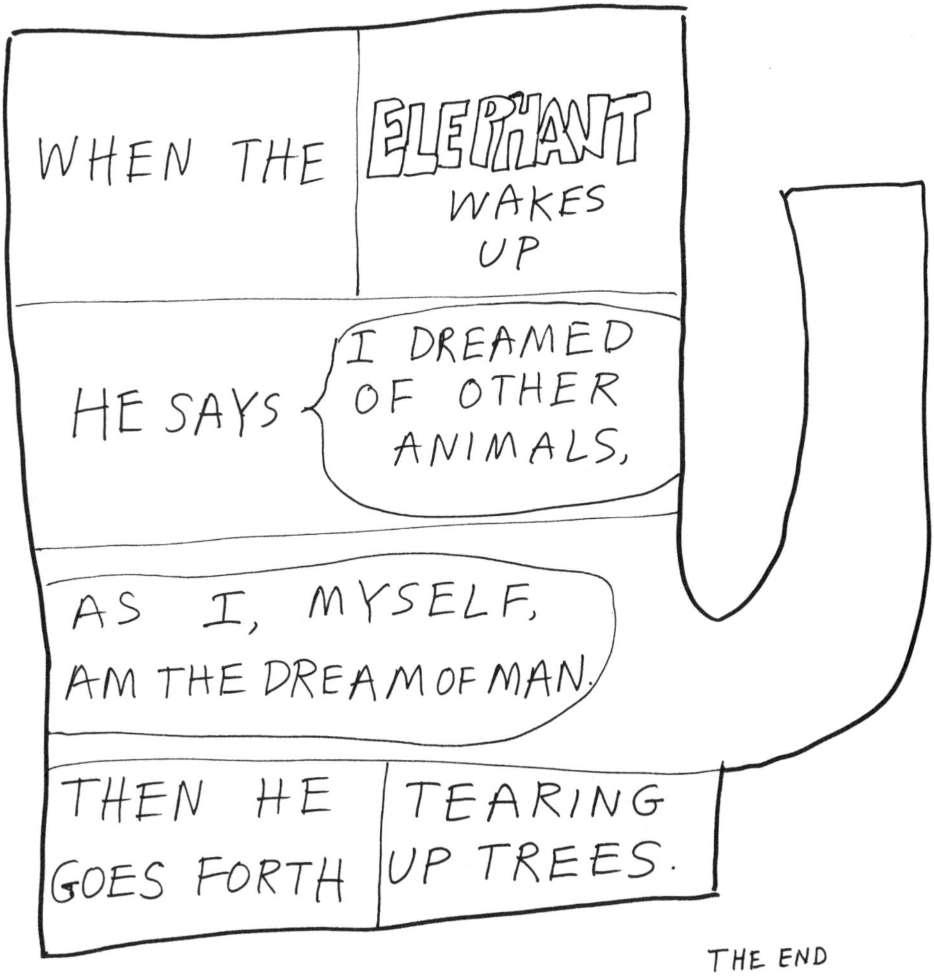
WHEN THE
ELEPHANT WAKES UP
HE SAYS
I DREAMED OF OTHER ANIMALS,
AS I, MYSELF, AM THE DREAM OF MAN.
THEN HE GOES FORTH
TEARING UP TREES.

THE END

FLAGS OF DIFFERENT NATIONS

COMICS

U.S.A.

FRANCE

ENGLAND

ITALY

MEXICO

SPAIN

CHINA

JAPAN

SWEDEN

TURKEY

GOWANALAND

OLD KISSING MAN comics

O BEAUTIFUL COMICS OF MY HEART

WITH BREASTS LIKE ORANGES

GIVE ME ONE KISS ERE I DEPART

TO END	MY DAYS	IN	FLORIDA!

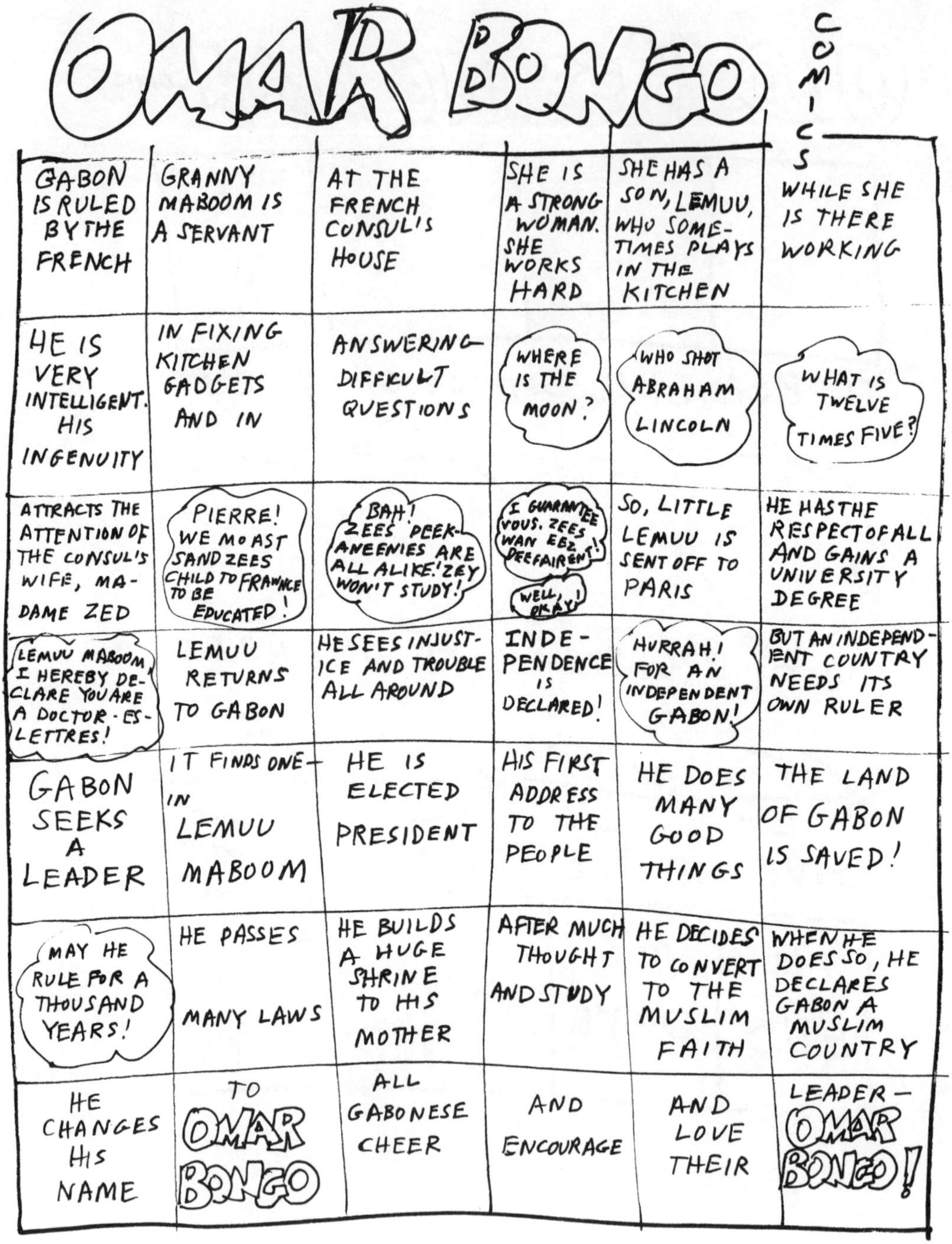
OMAR BONGO COMICS
GABON IS RULED BY THE FRENCH
GRANNY MABOOM IS A SERVANT
AT THE FRENCH CONSUL'S HOUSE
SHE IS A STRONG WOMAN. SHE WORKS HARD
SHE HAS A SON, LEMUU, WHO SOMETIMES PLAYS IN THE KITCHEN
WHILE SHE IS THERE WORKING
HE IS VERY INTELLIGENT. HIS INGENUITY
IN FIXING KITCHEN GADGETS AND IN
ANSWERING DIFFICULT QUESTIONS
WHERE IS THE MOON?
WHO SHOT ABRAHAM LINCOLN
WHAT IS TWELVE TIMES FIVE?
ATTRACTS THE ATTENTION OF THE CONSUL'S WIFE, MADAME ZED
PIERRE! WE MOAST SAND ZEES CHILD TO FRANCE TO BE EDUCATED!
BAH! ZEES PEEKANEENIES ARE ALL ALIKE! ZEY WON'T STUDY!
I GUARANTEE VOUS. ZEES WAN EEZ DEEFAIRENT!
WELL, OKAY!
SO, LITTLE LEMUU IS SENT OFF TO PARIS
HE HAS THE RESPECT OF ALL AND GAINS A UNIVERSITY DEGREE
LEMUU MABOOM, I HEREBY DECLARE YOU ARE A DOCTOR-ES-LETTRES!
LEMUU RETURNS TO GABON
HE SEES INJUSTICE AND TROUBLE ALL AROUND
INDEPENDENCE IS DECLARED!
HURRAH! FOR AN INDEPENDENT GABON!
BUT AN INDEPENDENT COUNTRY NEEDS ITS OWN RULER
GABON SEEKS A LEADER
IT FINDS ONE— IN LEMUU MABOOM
HE IS ELECTED PRESIDENT
HIS FIRST ADDRESS TO THE PEOPLE
HE DOES MANY GOOD THINGS
THE LAND OF GABON IS SAVED!
MAY HE RULE FOR A THOUSAND YEARS!
HE PASSES MANY LAWS
HE BUILDS A HUGE SHRINE TO HIS MOTHER
AFTER MUCH THOUGHT AND STUDY
HE DECIDES TO CONVERT TO THE MUSLIM FAITH
WHEN HE DOES SO, HE DECLARES GABON A MUSLIM COUNTRY
HE CHANGES HIS NAME
TO OMAR BONGO
ALL GABONESE CHEER
AND ENCOURAGE
AND LOVE THEIR
LEADER— OMAR BONGO!

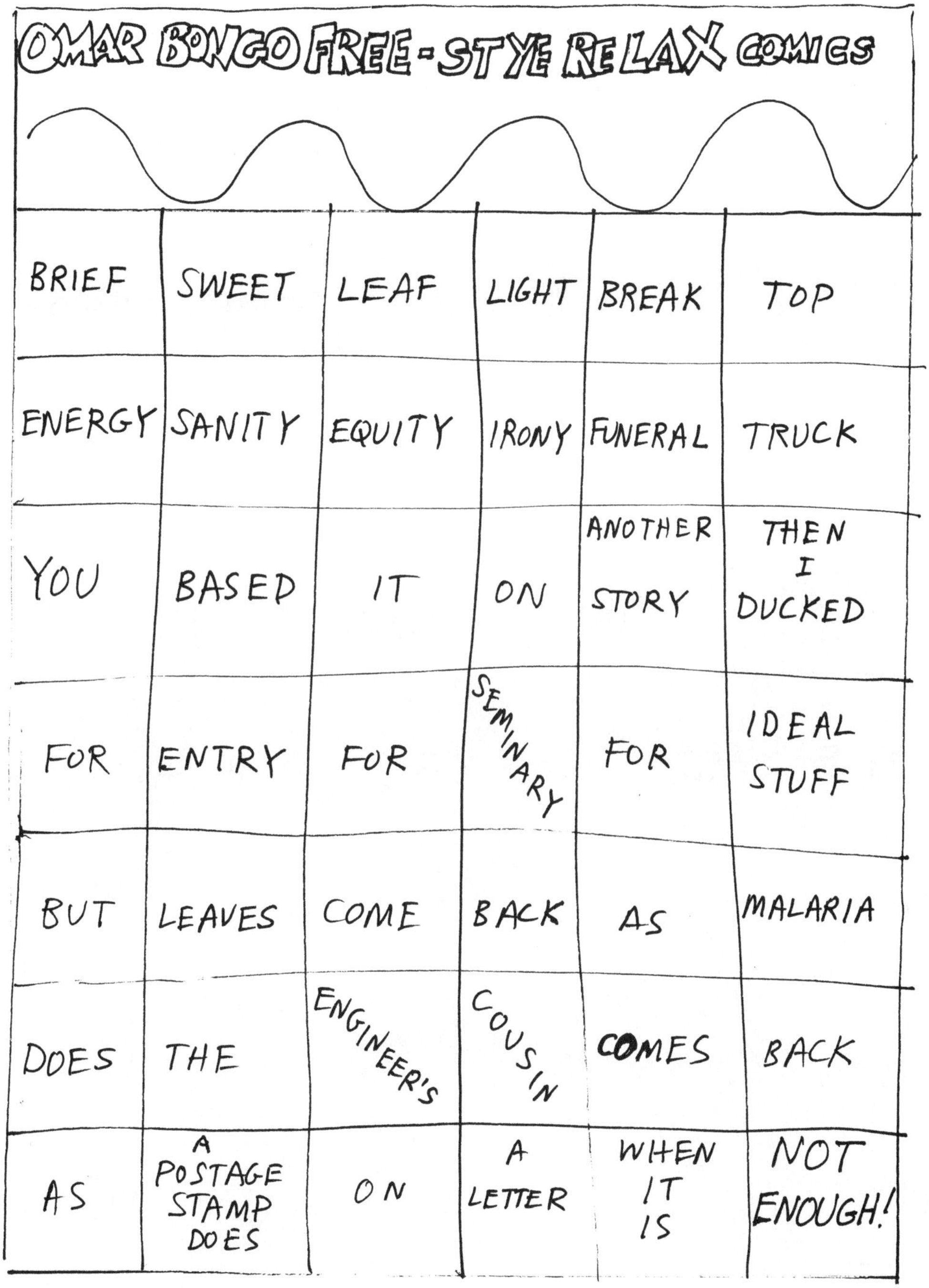

BRIEF	SWEET	LEAF	LIGHT	BREAK	TOP
ENERGY	SANITY	EQUITY	IRONY	FUNERAL	TRUCK
YOU	BASED	IT	ON	ANOTHER STORY	THEN I DUCKED
FOR	ENTRY	FOR	SEMINARY	FOR	IDEAL STUFF
BUT	LEAVES	COME	BACK	AS	MALARIA
DOES	THE	ENGINEER'S	COUSIN	COMES	BACK
AS	A POSTAGE STAMP DOES	ON	A LETTER	WHEN IT IS	NOT ENOUGH!

BONGO FREE-STYLE RELAX

OMAR

COMICS

NUMBER TWO

AND	SO	THE	ROAD	CAME	BACK
TOO	INTO	COMICS	HER-ALDED	BY	ALL
KINDS	OF	ROUGH	ELE-MENTS	THAT	SAVED
THE	TREES	OF	THE	RAIN	FOREST
RUST	AND	TRAIN	BUT	SHEAVES	A CUFF
EX-PLAIN	THE ROUGH	UN-ENTERED	STRAIN	SEEK-ING	IT
BEFORE	REIN-FORCING	IT	AS IF	THE WAVES	THEN

34

DEER TENDON COMICS

TEN PERSONS —FOUR MEN AND SIX WOMEN—	SIT DOWN TO A LITTLE "BANQUET" IN KUNMING, CHINA	KUNMING HAS A YEAR-ROUND PLEASANT SPRINGTIME CLIMATE OF ABOUT SIXTY SEVEN DEGREES
FARENHEIT	MANY THINGS ARE SERVED: SHREDDED COCONUT, BAMBOO SHOOTS WITH PEANUT SAUCE, SKY ONIONS, "BATTERED" RICE	THEN COMES THE "MAIN" OR "SPECIAL" COURSE (FOR WHICH THIS BANQUET IS NAMED)
SUSPENSE AS THE WAITER BRINGS IT IN AND SETS IT DOWN	WO LANIU, AS GUEST OF HONOR, UN- COVERS THE DISH. "WHAT IS IT?"	DEER TENDON
ROBERTO, AFTERWARDS, SAYS, "IT WAS NOT TILL I WAS WELL INTO MY THIRD OR FOURTH BITE	OF THIS RUBBERY AND SOMEWHAT FLAT-TASTING THING THAT I REALIZED	WHAT IT PROBABLY WAS: DEER PENIS!" BETTY SAYS "OH MY GOD!"

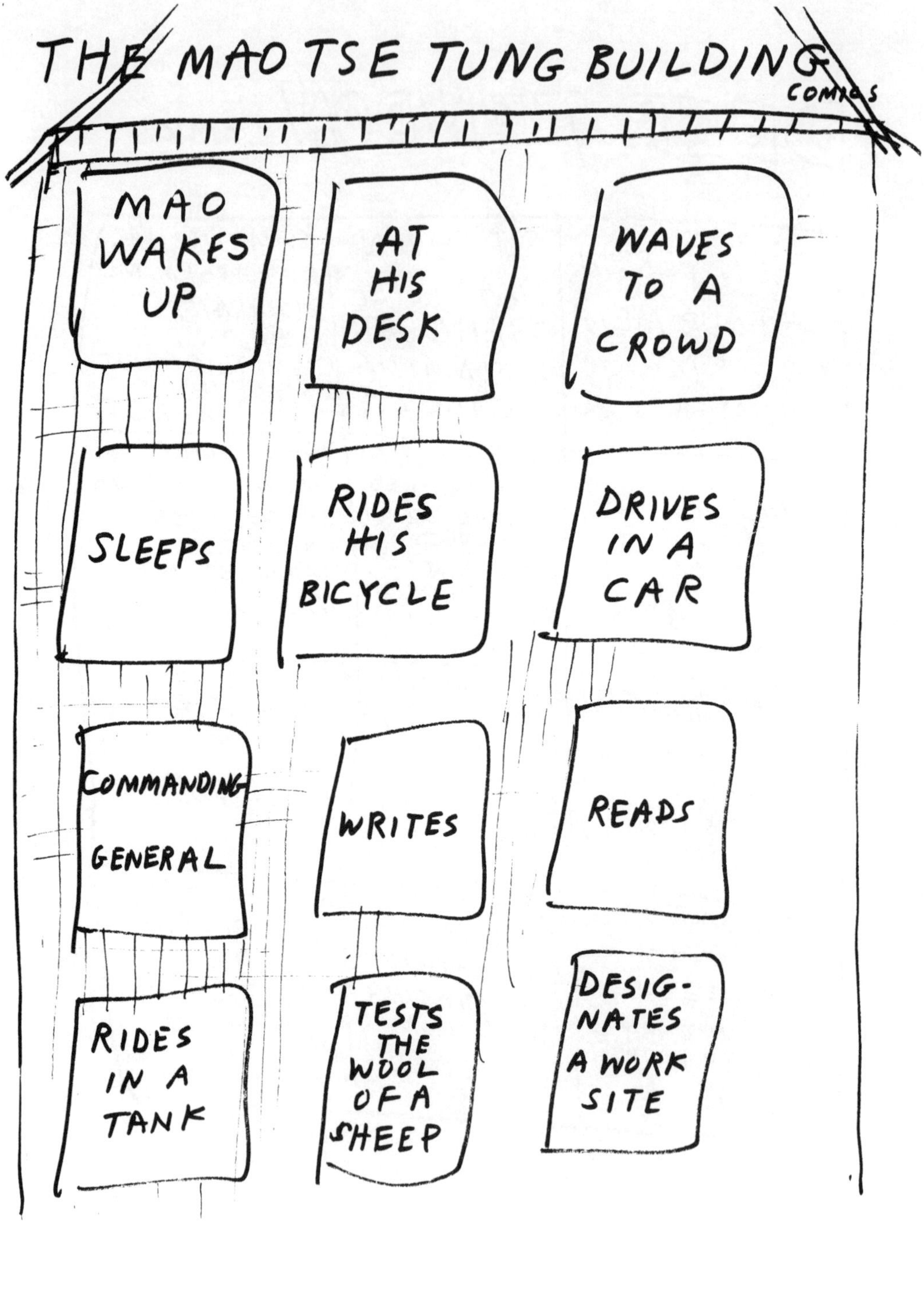
THE MAO TSE TUNG BUILDING
COMICS
MAO WAKES UP
AT HIS DESK
WAVES TO A CROWD
SLEEPS
RIDES HIS BICYCLE
DRIVES IN A CAR
COMMANDING GENERAL
WRITES
READS
RIDES IN A TANK
TESTS THE WOOL OF A SHEEP
DESIG-NATES A WORK SITE

MAO TSE TUNG OUTSIDE HIS BUILDING

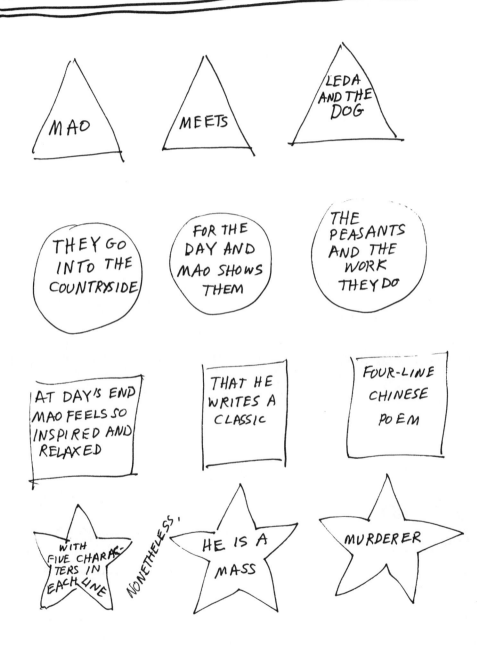

MAO

MEETS

LEDA AND THE DOG

THEY GO INTO THE COUNTRYSIDE

FOR THE DAY AND MAO SHOWS THEM

THE PEASANTS AND THE WORK THEY DO

AT DAY'S END MAO FEELS SO INSPIRED AND RELAXED

THAT HE WRITES A CLASSIC

FOUR-LINE CHINESE POEM

WITH FIVE CHARAC-TERS IN EACH LINE

NONETHELESS,

HE IS A MASS

MURDERER

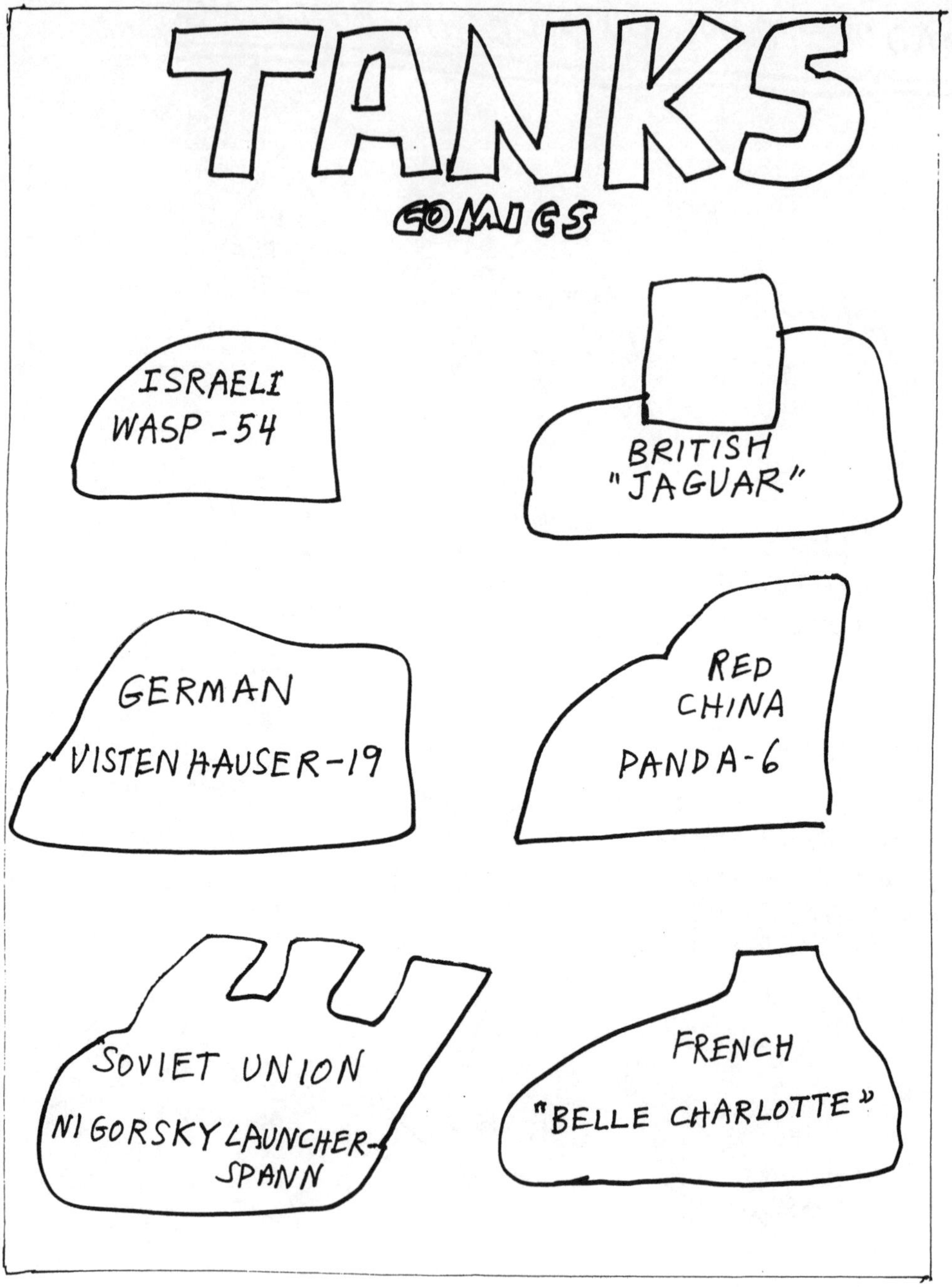
TANKS
COMICS
ISRAELI
WASP-54
BRITISH
"JAGUAR"
GERMAN
VISTENHAUSER-19
RED
CHINA
PANDA-6
SOVIET UNION
NIGORSKY LAUNCHER-
SPANN
FRENCH
"BELLE CHARLOTTE"

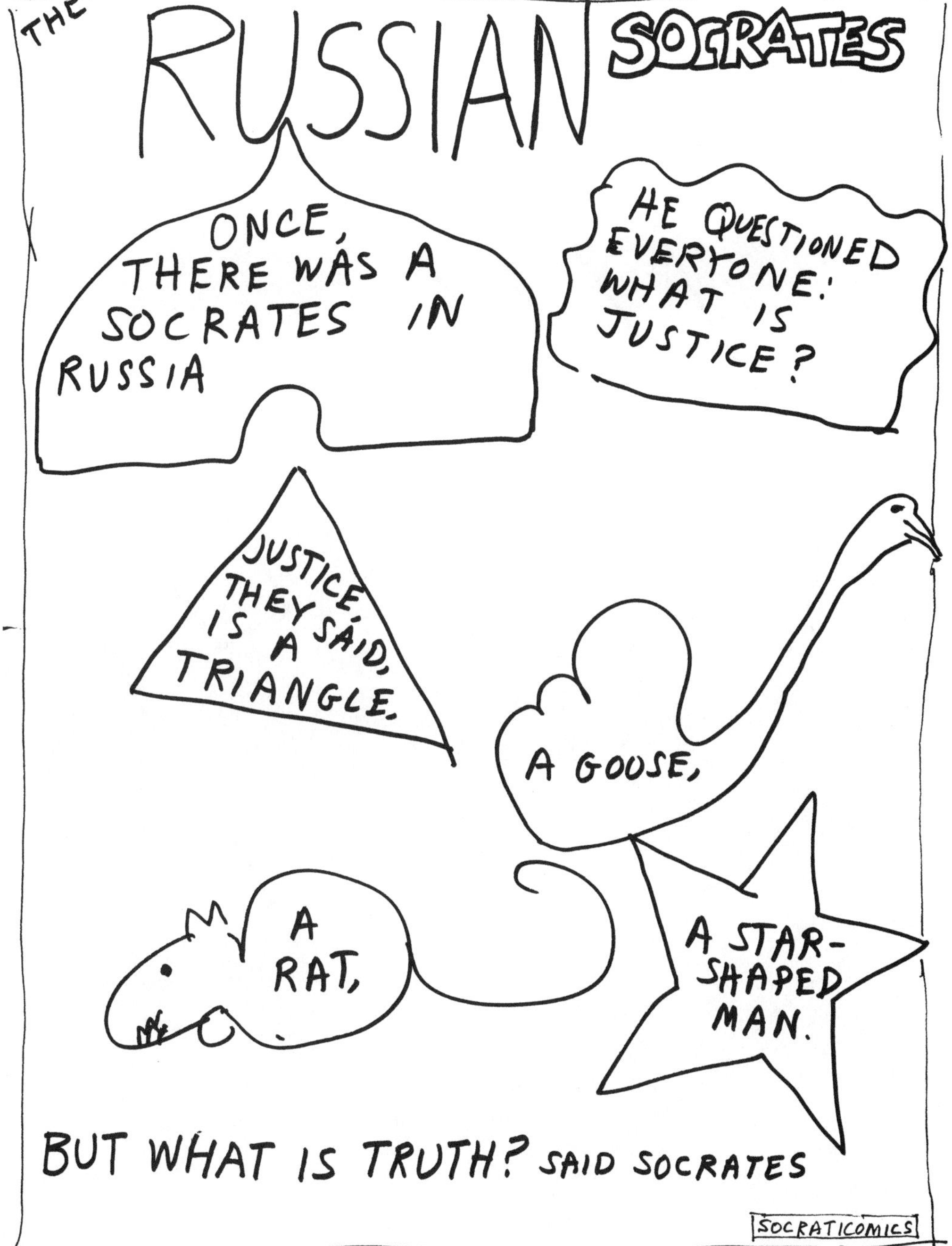
THE RUSSIAN SOCRATES
ONCE, THERE WAS A SOCRATES IN RUSSIA
HE QUESTIONED EVERYONE: WHAT IS JUSTICE?
JUSTICE, THEY SAID, IS A TRIANGLE.
A GOOSE,
A RAT,
A STAR-SHAPED MAN.
BUT WHAT IS TRUTH? SAID SOCRATES
SOCRATICOMICS

MASKED HAND
COMICS

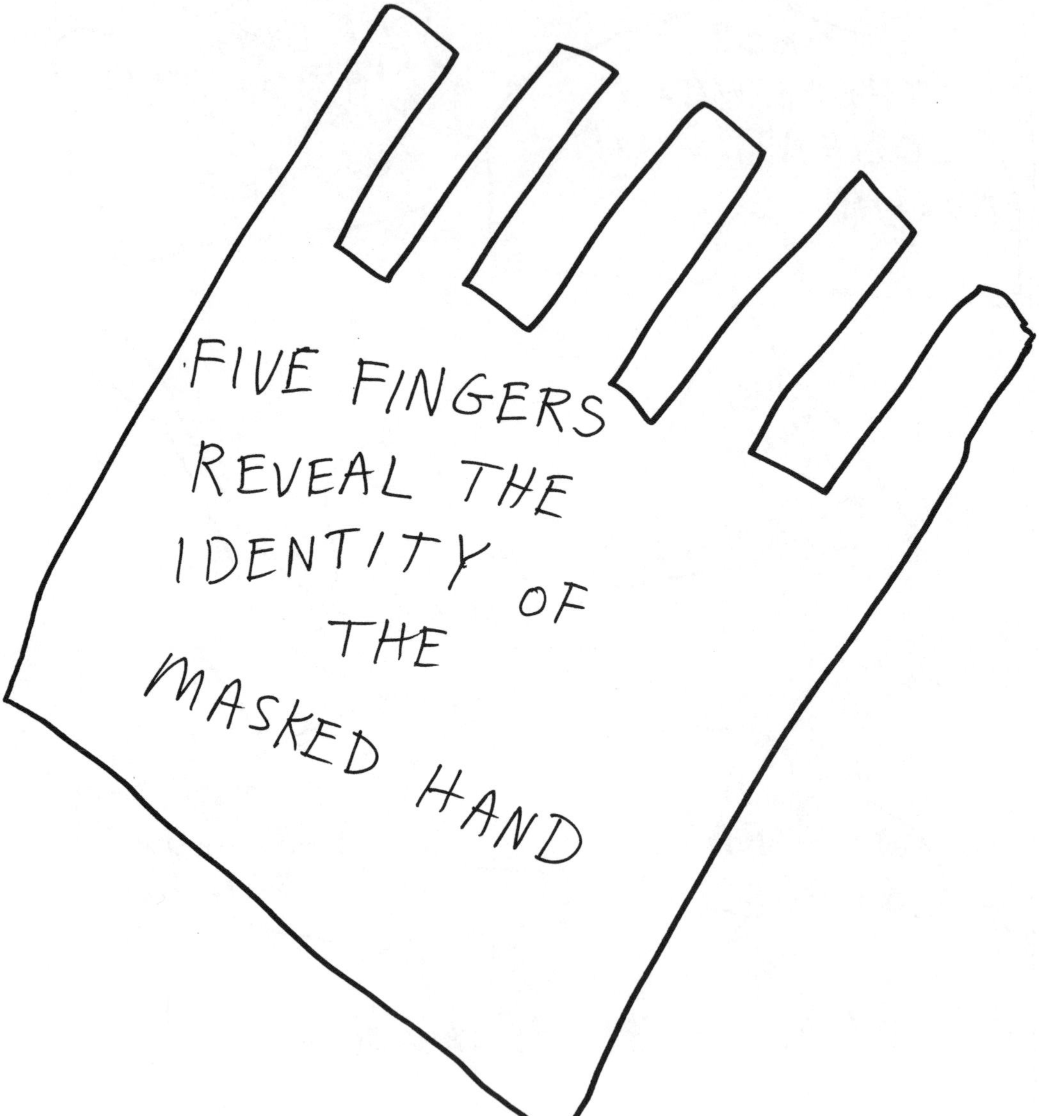
FIVE FINGERS
REVEAL THE
IDENTITY OF
THE
MASKED HAND

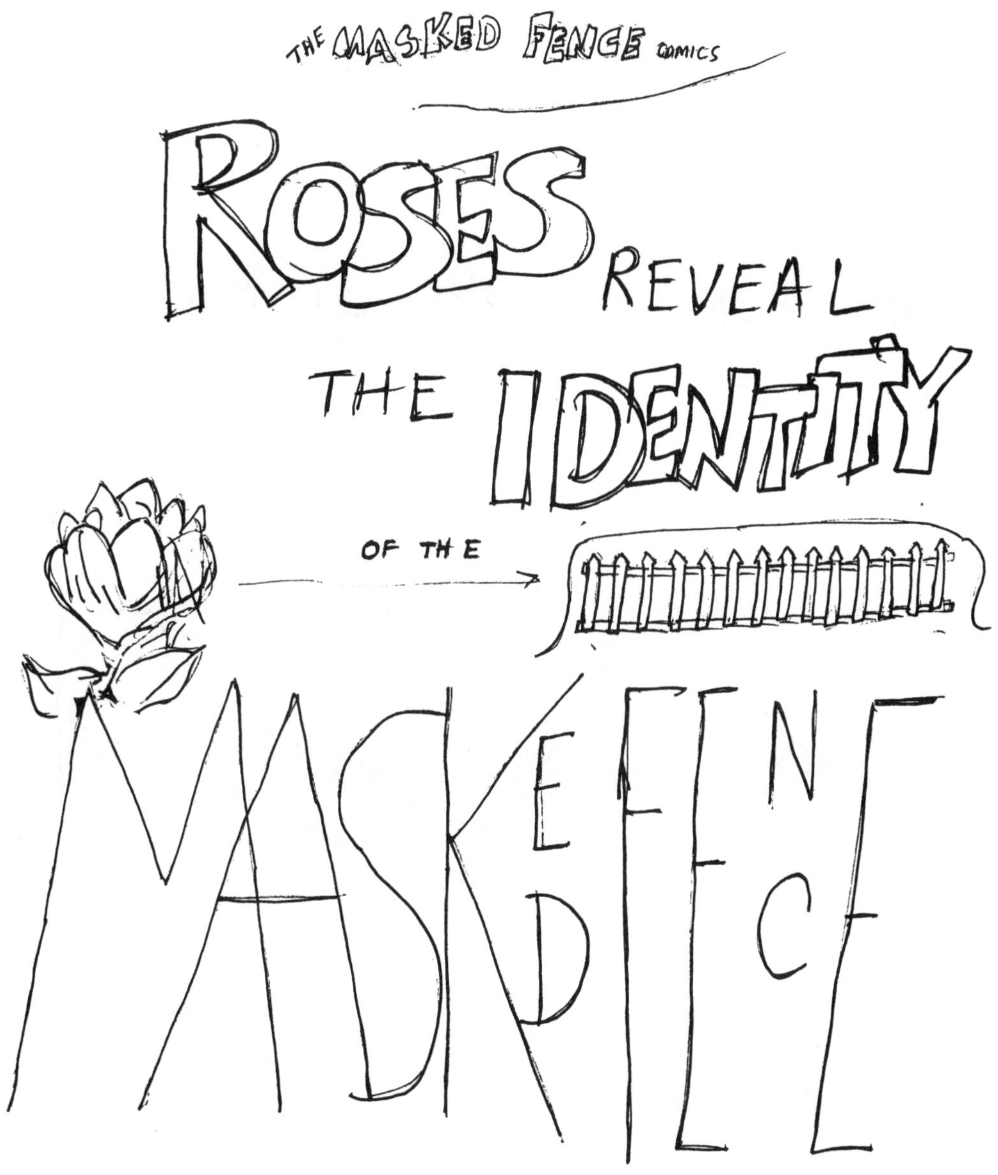
THE MASKED FENCE COMICS
ROSES REVEAL THE IDENTITY
OF THE
MASKED FENCE
COMICS

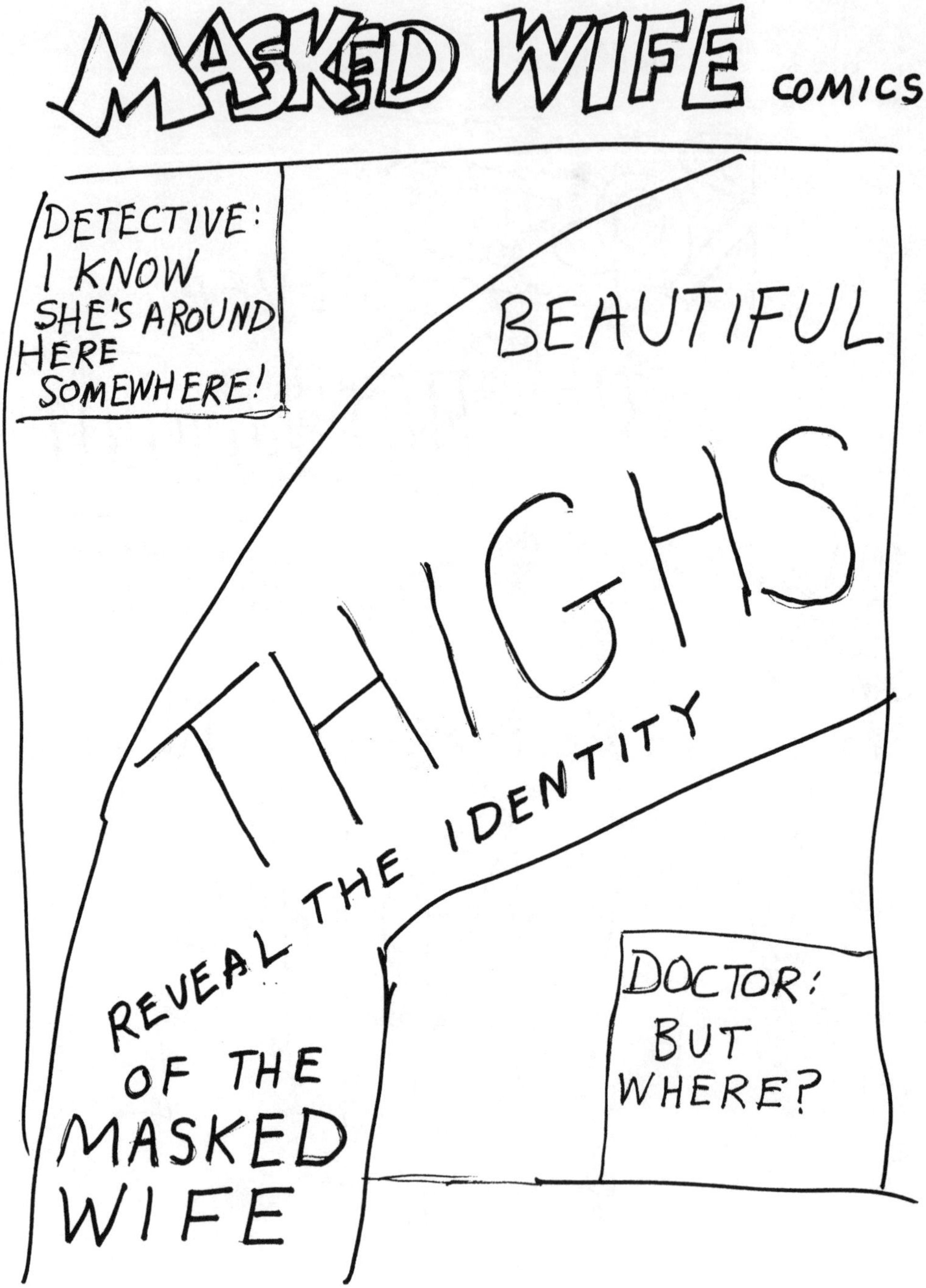
MASKED WIFE COMICS
DETECTIVE: I KNOW SHE'S AROUND HERE SOMEWHERE!
BEAUTIFUL
THIGHS
REVEAL THE IDENTITY
OF THE MASKED WIFE
DOCTOR: BUT WHERE?

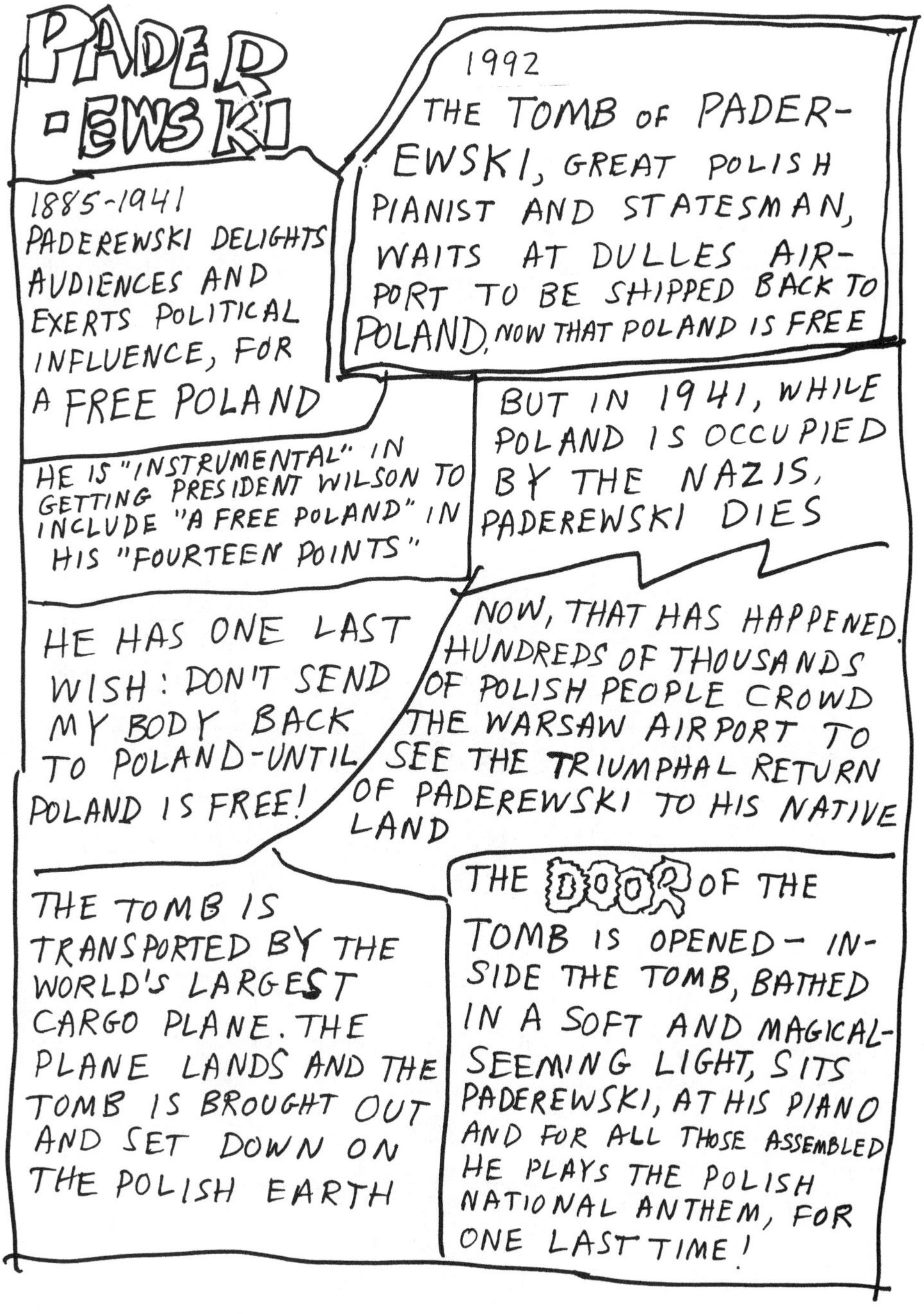
PADER-EWSKI
1885-1941
PADEREWSKI DELIGHTS AUDIENCES AND EXERTS POLITICAL INFLUENCE, FOR A FREE POLAND
1992
THE TOMB OF PADEREWSKI, GREAT POLISH PIANIST AND STATESMAN, WAITS AT DULLES AIRPORT TO BE SHIPPED BACK TO POLAND, NOW THAT POLAND IS FREE
HE IS "INSTRUMENTAL" IN GETTING PRESIDENT WILSON TO INCLUDE "A FREE POLAND" IN HIS "FOURTEEN POINTS"
BUT IN 1941, WHILE POLAND IS OCCUPIED BY THE NAZIS, PADEREWSKI DIES
HE HAS ONE LAST WISH: DON'T SEND MY BODY BACK TO POLAND-UNTIL POLAND IS FREE!
NOW, THAT HAS HAPPENED. HUNDREDS OF THOUSANDS OF POLISH PEOPLE CROWD THE WARSAW AIRPORT TO SEE THE TRIUMPHAL RETURN OF PADEREWSKI TO HIS NATIVE LAND
THE TOMB IS TRANSPORTED BY THE WORLD'S LARGEST CARGO PLANE. THE PLANE LANDS AND THE TOMB IS BROUGHT OUT AND SET DOWN ON THE POLISH EARTH
THE DOOR OF THE TOMB IS OPENED - INSIDE THE TOMB, BATHED IN A SOFT AND MAGICAL-SEEMING LIGHT, SITS PADEREWSKI, AT HIS PIANO AND FOR ALL THOSE ASSEMBLED HE PLAYS THE POLISH NATIONAL ANTHEM, FOR ONE LAST TIME!

MADAME DE LAFAYETTE

BORN	INTO	THE	FRENCH	ARISTO-CRACY
JEANNE	ELYSIE	DE LA CLOS	MET	AND
MARRIED	THE	DUKE	OF	PONCE
MONSIEUR	DE LAFAYETTE	SHE	WROTE	A
VERY	GREAT	BOOK	WHICH	IS
CALLED	LA	PRINCESSE	DE	CLÈVES

OR   THE   PRINCESS   OF   CLÈVES

LATER			
	WHEN SHE		
		HAD A	LITTLE

MADAME DE LAFAYETTE 2

TIME TO			
THINK	ABOUT IT		
SHE SAID	ZOWIE!	JE	L'AI ÉCRIT!

HOTEL IGURA comics

ROOM SEVEN NINETEEN	OF THE HOTEL IGURA	IN SAPPORO	A MAN CLINGS	TO AN OLD IDEA
HE WANTS TO THROW IT OUT	BUT THERE IS NO WINDOW	THAT OPENS	HE WANTS	TO THROW WHAT OUT?
A TOWEL	NAKED WITH DREAMS	AND SHE	IS YOUNG, VERY YOUNG	YOUNGEST
FEET THRASH ABOUT	THE HOTEL'S SURFACE	NOW HE IS SETTLING DOWN	WHO? THE SUN	SIX P.M. SIX FIF- TEEN, EVEN
A GIRL SAYS NOW	I'M SORRY	I CAN'T DO THAT	BUT I HAVE A BOY FRIEND	SERIOUS, A FIANCÉ
WHY DID THESE BELT-BUCK- LE	SOAP THREE	WE HEARD THE ELEVATOR	GRASPING AT FLOORS	COARSE SPENDING
YOU'LL NEED A DIRECTOR	IF YOU WANT TO DO A PLAY	TOMORROW THE	NEXT ONE	EVENING HOTEL

46

UNFOLDING THE MATTRESS COMICS

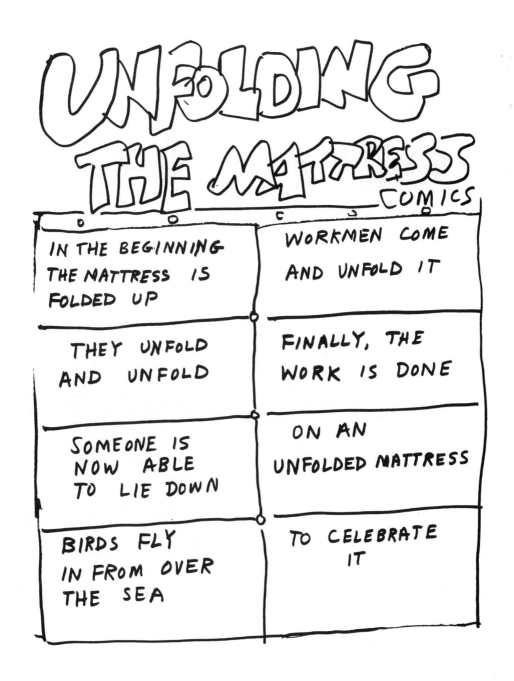

IN THE BEGINNING THE MATTRESS IS FOLDED UP	WORKMEN COME AND UNFOLD IT
THEY UNFOLD AND UNFOLD	FINALLY, THE WORK IS DONE
SOMEONE IS NOW ABLE TO LIE DOWN	ON AN UNFOLDED MATTRESS
BIRDS FLY IN FROM OVER THE SEA	TO CELEBRATE IT

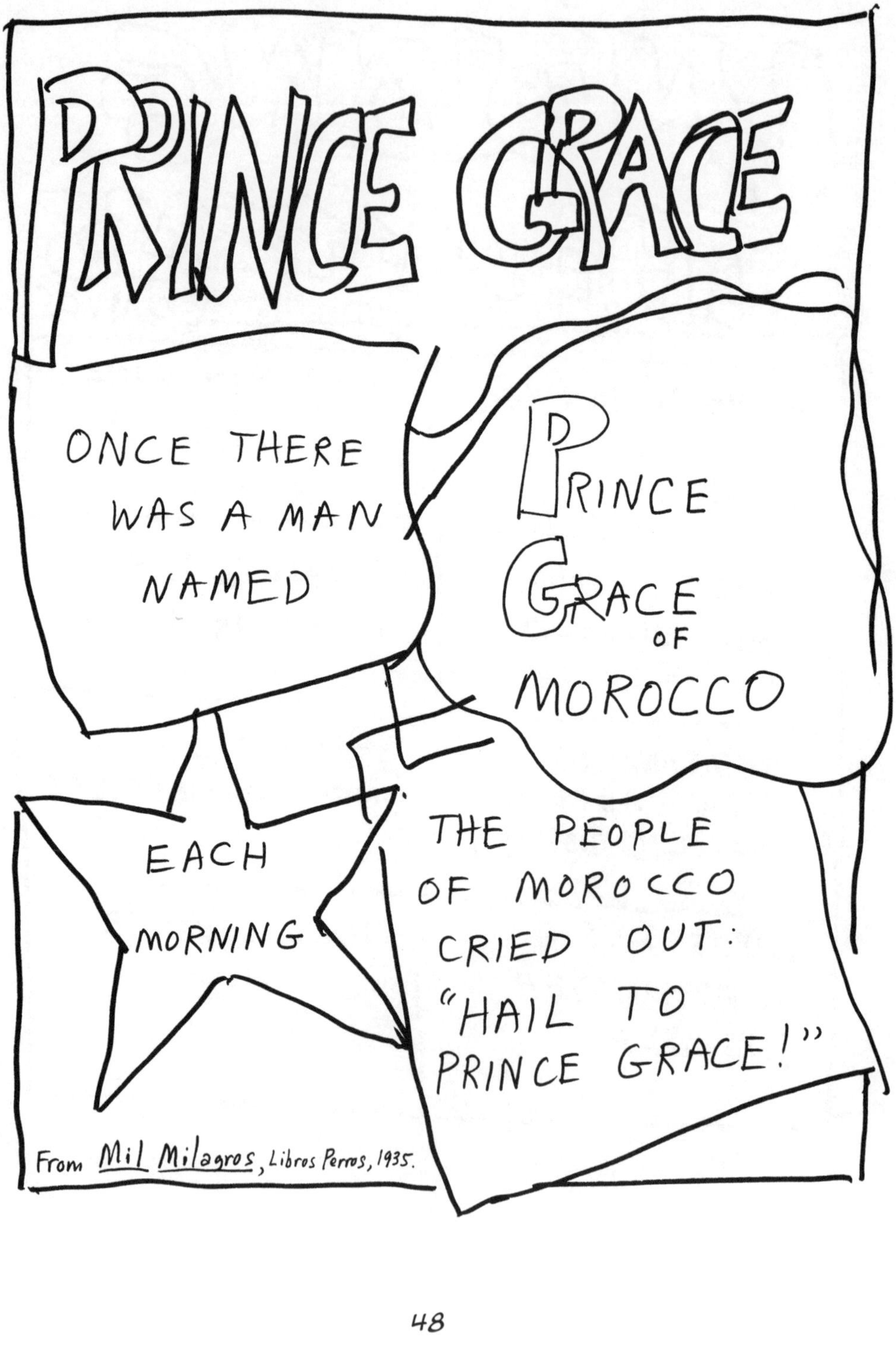
PRINCE GRACE
ONCE THERE WAS A MAN NAMED
PRINCE GRACE OF MOROCCO
EACH MORNING
THE PEOPLE OF MOROCCO CRIED OUT: "HAIL TO PRINCE GRACE!"
From Mil Milagros, Libros Perros, 1935.

PURE COMICS

Pure

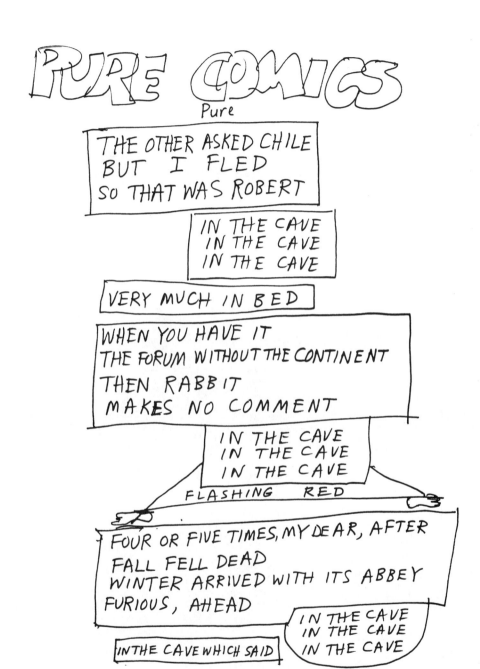

THE OTHER ASKED CHILE
BUT I FLED
SO THAT WAS ROBERT

IN THE CAVE
IN THE CAVE
IN THE CAVE

VERY MUCH IN BED

WHEN YOU HAVE IT
THE FORUM WITHOUT THE CONTINENT
THEN RABBIT
MAKES NO COMMENT

IN THE CAVE
IN THE CAVE
IN THE CAVE

FLASHING RED

FOUR OR FIVE TIMES, MY DEAR, AFTER
FALL FELL DEAD
WINTER ARRIVED WITH ITS ABBEY
FURIOUS, AHEAD

IN THE CAVE WHICH SAID

IN THE CAVE
IN THE CAVE
IN THE CAVE

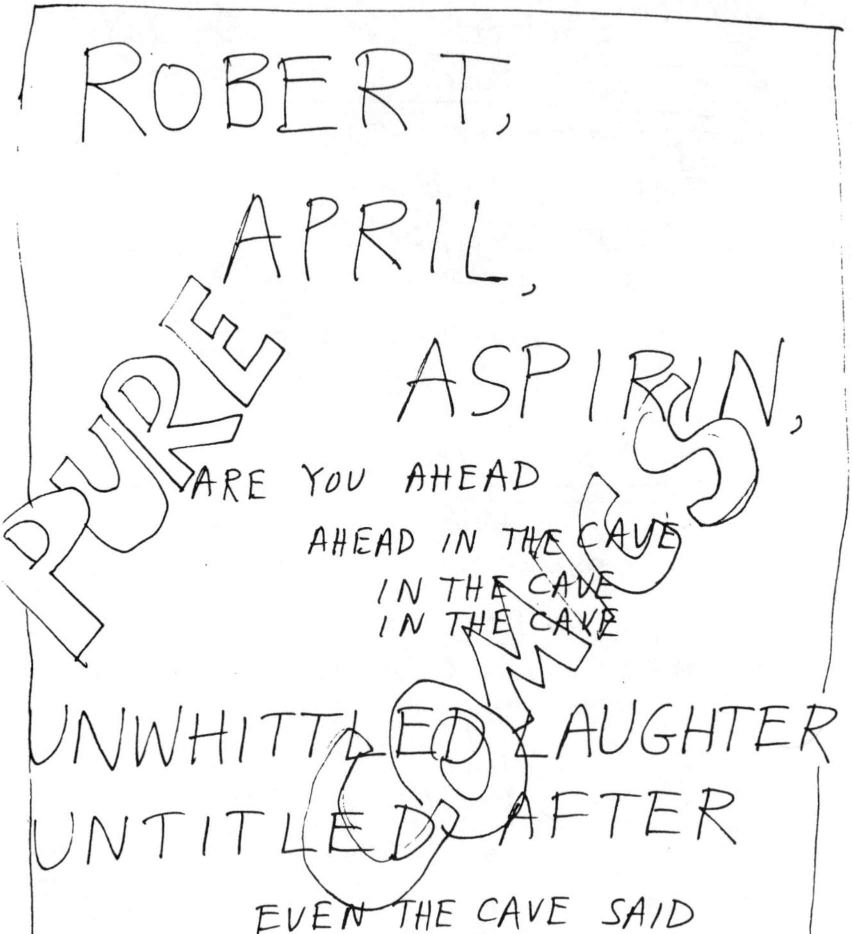
ROBERT,
APRIL,
ASPIRIN,
ARE YOU AHEAD
AHEAD IN THE CAVE
IN THE CAVE
IN THE CAVE
UNWHITTLED LAUGHTER
UNTITLED AFTER
EVEN THE CAVE SAID
ASPIRIN, APRIL, GLOW
PURE COMICS

PUZZLE PAGE

FIND THE MOOSE

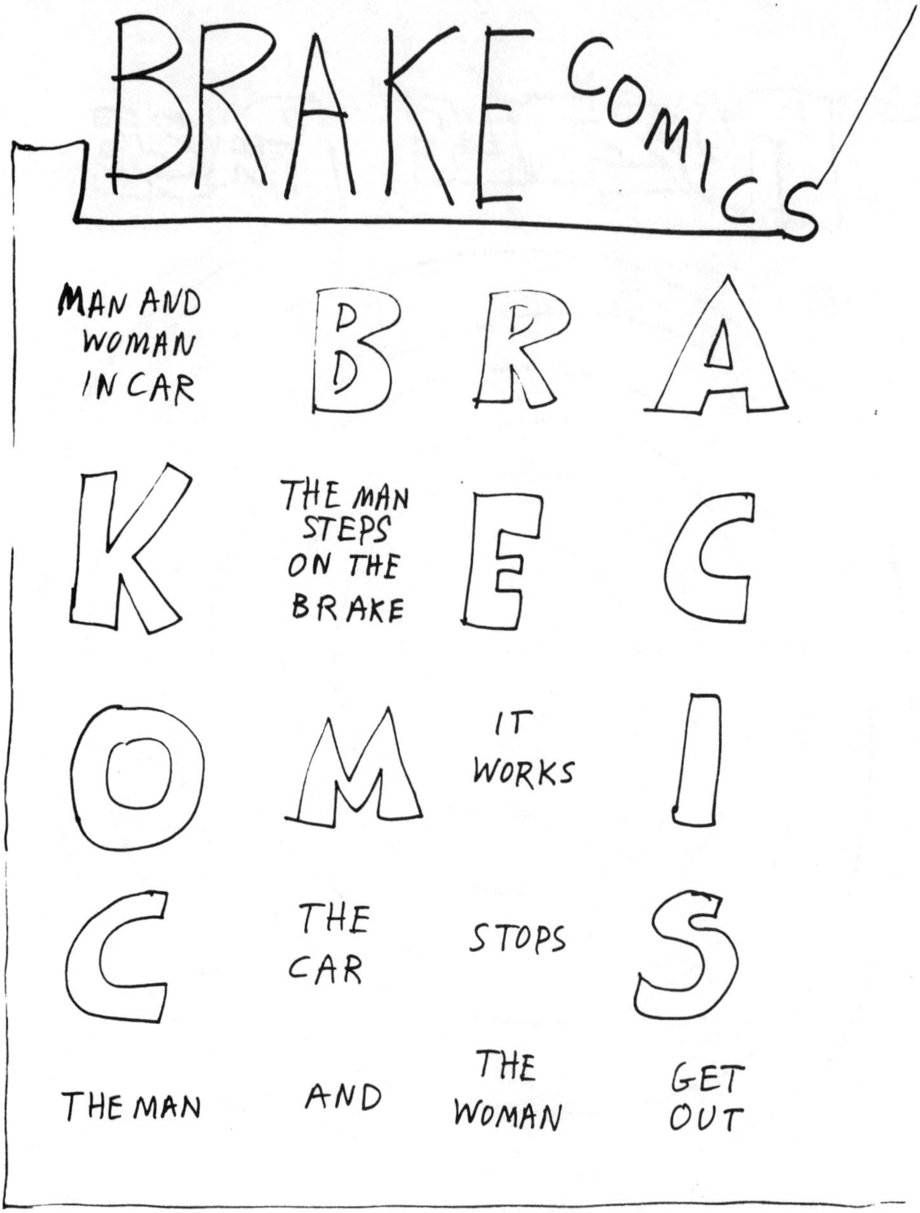
BRAKE COMICS
MAN AND WOMAN IN CAR
B R A
K
THE MAN STEPS ON THE BRAKE
E C
O M
IT WORKS
I
C
THE CAR
STOPS
S
THE MAN
AND
THE WOMAN
GET OUT

BIRTH COMICS

A BABY IS BORN	SHE IS NAMED "ANGELA"	THE MOTHER HOLDS HER	ANGELA WAVES ONE FAT HAND
THE MOTHER TAKES THIS HAND IN HER OWN HAND	ANGELA TURNS TOWARD HER MOTHER	HER MOTHER'S BREAST	ANGELA IS FED
THE MOTHER MEETS A MAN	WHO BECOMES THE FATHER	OF BABY ANGELA	"HELLO!" HE SAYS
HE DANCES WITH HER	THE PAIN IS INTENSE. HE HOLDS HER HAND.	THE PHYSICIAN: IT'S A GIRL!	NOW ANGELA FALLS ASLEEP
HER FATHER COMES HOME	HE KISSES HIS WIFE	HOW IS ANGELA?	HIS WIFE SAYS "SHE'S ASLEEP!"

DON'T SPOIL IT

A MAN CARRIES IN A WATERMELON	HE PLACES IT ON A TABLE	THE BABY IS ASLEEP
THE DOG IS OUTSIDE	A LIGHT BREEZE IS BLOWING	A WOMAN ENTERS THE ROOM
SHE WHIS-PERS "THE DOG IS OUTSIDE."	THE MAN SAYS, "OH."	THE WOMAN LOOKS IN A MIRROR AND SLIGHTLY RE-ARRANGES HER HAIR
THE MAN CALLS TO THE DOG OUTSIDE	"RUTGER, COME IN!" THE DOG BOUNDS PAST HIM	AND GOES TO HIS DISH AND DRINKS
THE SKY IS DARK WHITE-BLUE	ANGELA IS SMILING	DON'T SPOIL IT

APPLIQUÉ COMICS

HERE AND THERE A SPOT	OF **RED** IS APPLIQUÉ	ROB GETS OUT HIS FRENCH-ENGLISH DICTIONARY	IT'S HEAVY!
BOY! THIS WEIGHS A TON!	SO, BETTY SAYS, WHAT'S "APPLIQUÉ"?	IT MEANS "PUT ON" ROB SAYS	BETTY SITS DOWN
FLOWERED ARMCHAIR	FLOWERED ARMCHAIR	SMALL ROUND TABLE	FLOWERED ARMCHAIR
SEA	**SEA**	**SEA**	**SEA**
WINDOW	HAND LOTION	SHARK	CEMENT

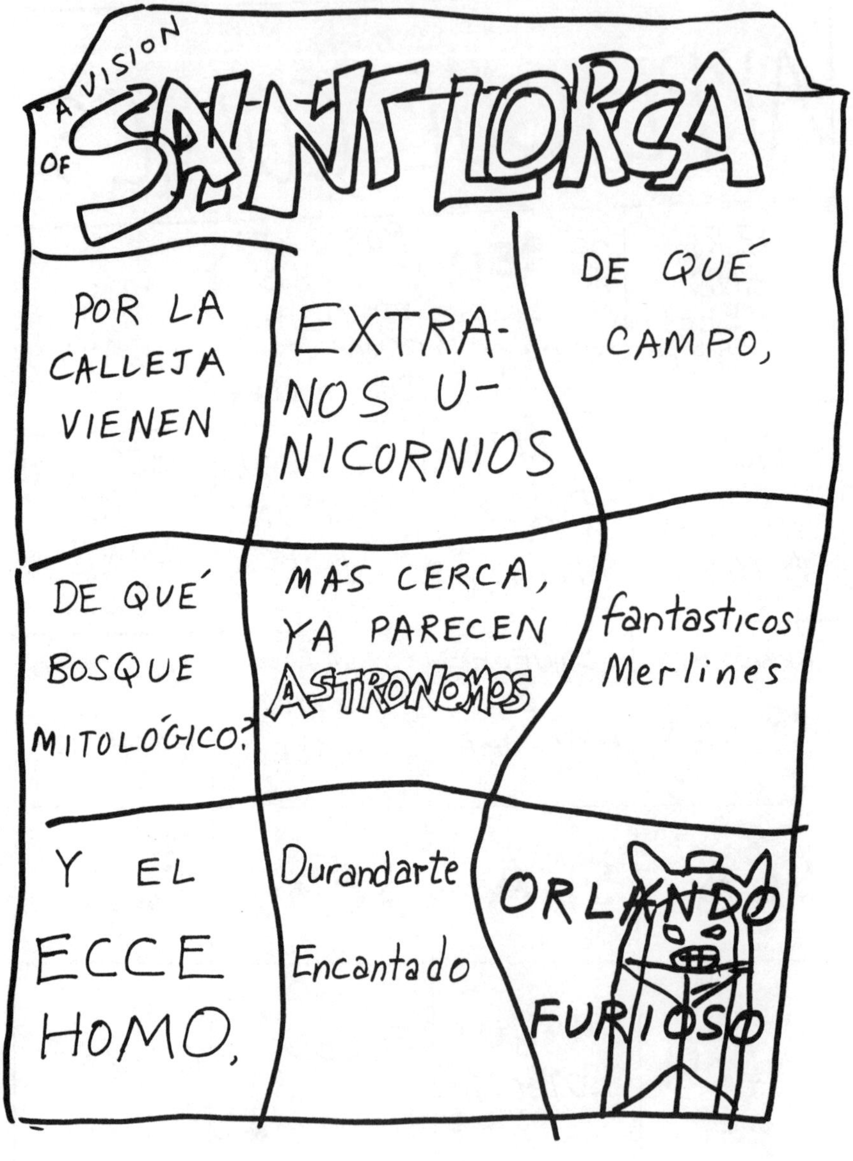
A VISION OF
SAINT LORCA
POR LA CALLEJA VIENEN
EXTRA-NOS U-NICORNIOS
DE QUÉ CAMPO,
DE QUÉ BOSQUE MITOLÓGICO?
MÁS CERCA, YA PARECEN
ASTRONOMOS
fantasticos Merlines
Y EL ECCE HOMO,
Durandarte Encantado
ORLANDO FURIOSO

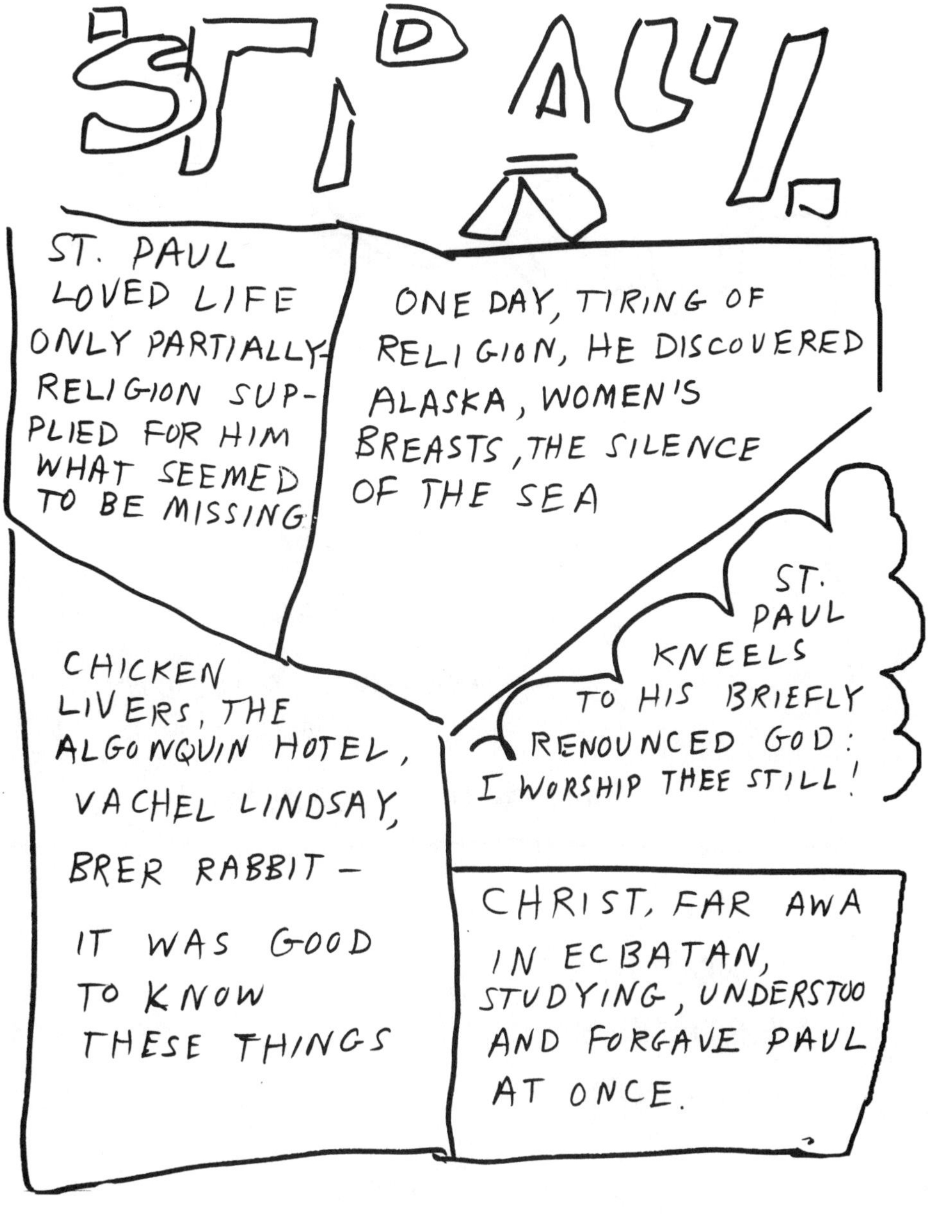
ST. PAUL
ST. PAUL LOVED LIFE ONLY PARTIALLY-RELIGION SUP-PLIED FOR HIM WHAT SEEMED TO BE MISSING:
ONE DAY, TIRING OF RELIGION, HE DISCOVERED ALASKA, WOMEN'S BREASTS, THE SILENCE OF THE SEA
CHICKEN LIVERS, THE ALGONQUIN HOTEL, VACHEL LINDSAY, BRER RABBIT – IT WAS GOOD TO KNOW THESE THINGS
ST. PAUL KNEELS TO HIS BRIEFLY RENOUNCED GOD: I WORSHIP THEE STILL!
CHRIST, FAR AWA IN ECBATAN, STUDYING, UNDERSTOO AND FORGAVE PAUL AT ONCE.

BUS COMICS

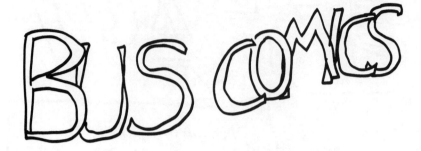

WHERE DOES THIS BUS GO?

AS FAR AS WITH YOU IN IT!

I DON'T UNDERSTAND!
GIVE ME THE HOOK OF THE DAY.

Parliament Grandstand

LADY:
CONDUCTOR:
LADY:
CONDUCTOR:

Evening hum

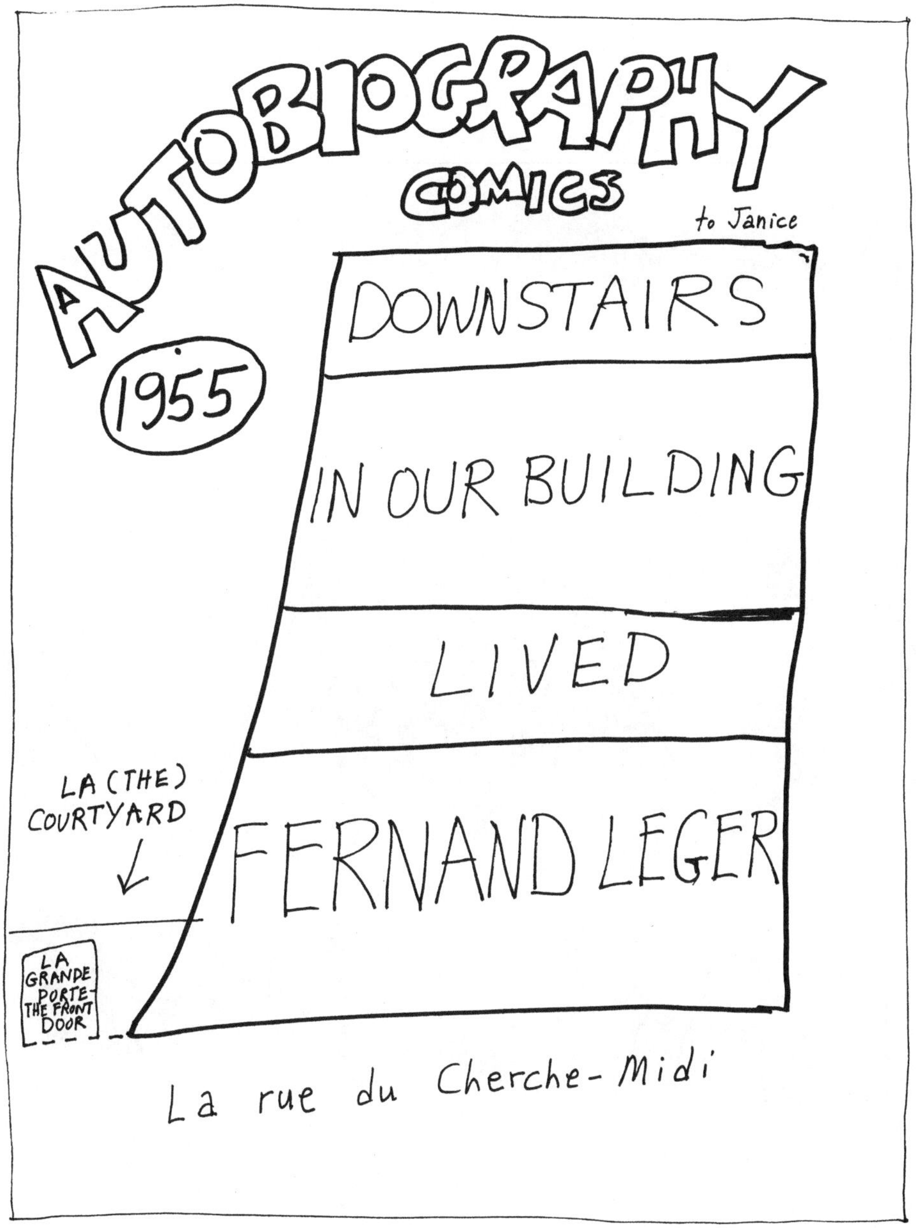

AUTOBIOGRAPHY COMICS
to Janice
1955
DOWNSTAIRS
IN OUR BUILDING
LIVED
FERNAND LEGER
LA (THE) COURTYARD
LA GRANDE PORTE- THE FRONT DOOR
La rue du Cherche-Midi

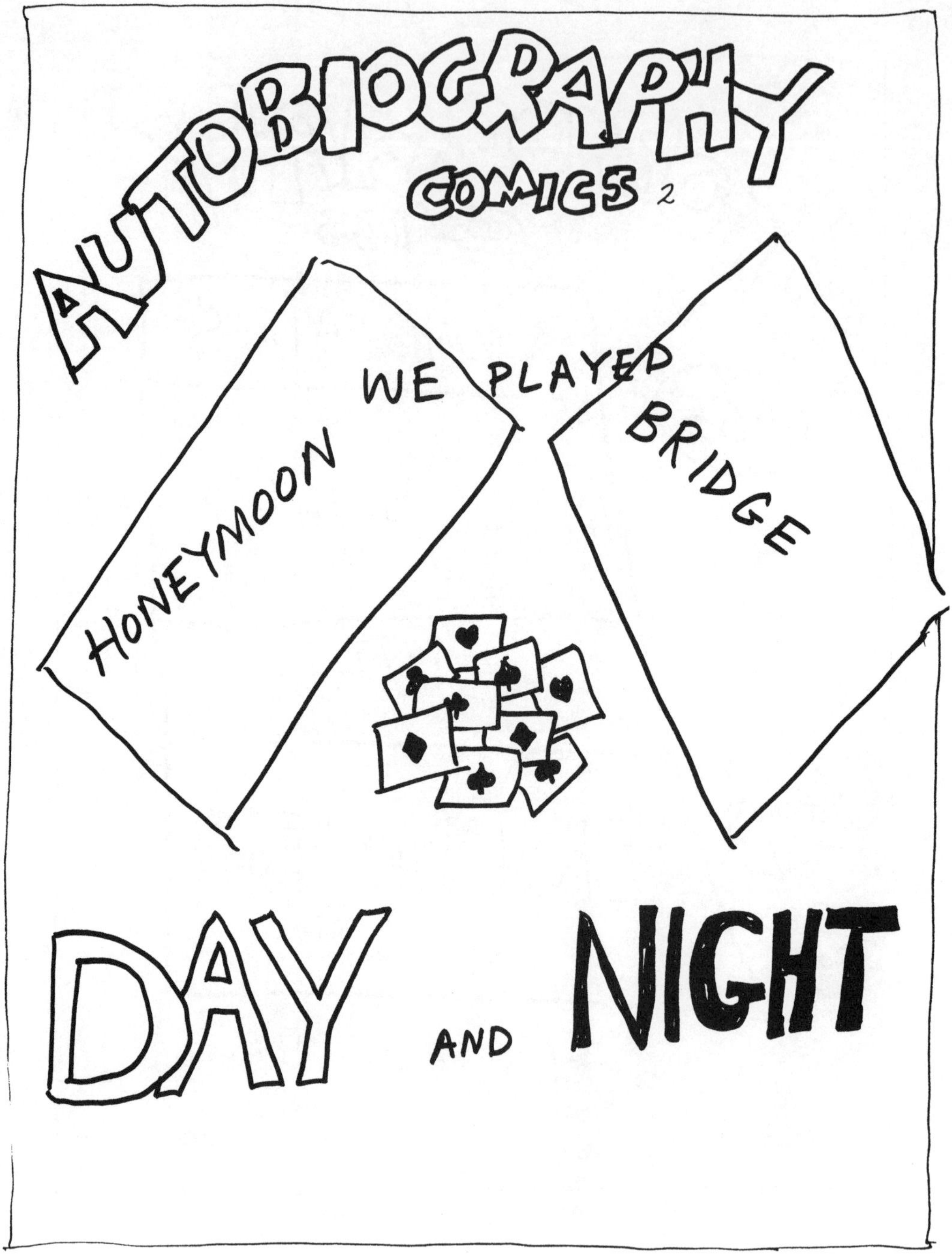
AUTOBIOGRAPHY COMICS 2
HONEYMOON WE PLAYED BRIDGE
DAY AND NIGHT

AUTOBIOGRAPHY
COMICS 3
WHEN THE
BABY
WAS BORN
WE
JUMPED
FOR JOY
AND AT
NINE MONTHS SHE
SANG
EACH
MORNING
IN HER CRIB

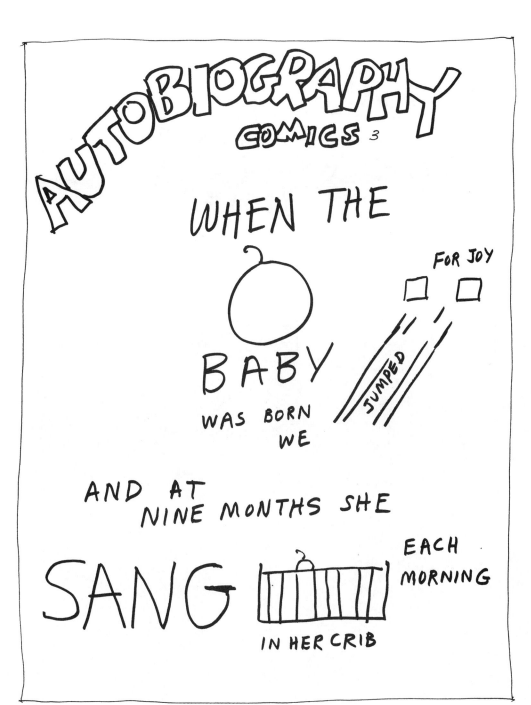

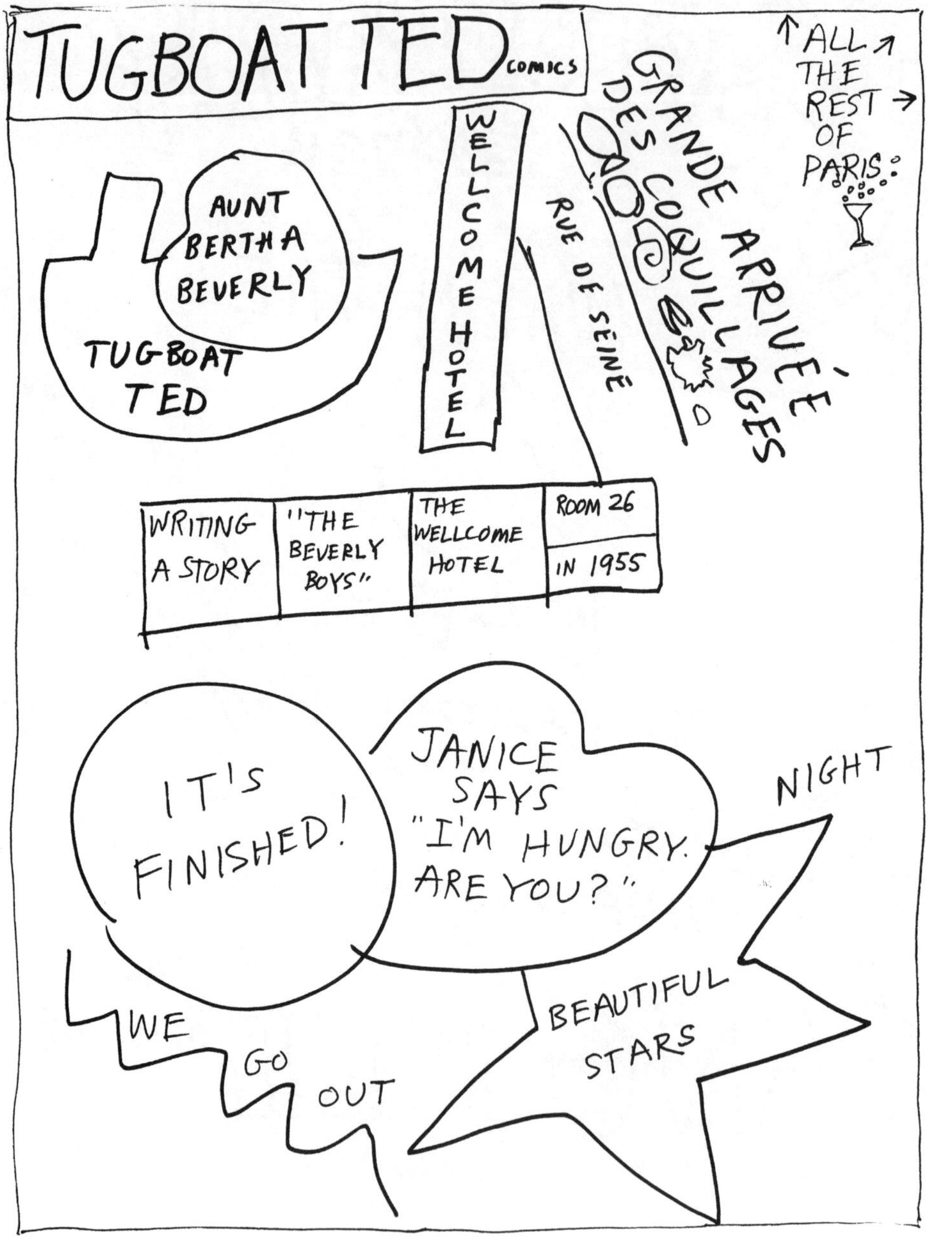
TUGBOAT TED COMICS
AUNT BERTHA BEVERLY
TUGBOAT TED
WELLCOME HOTEL
RUE DE SEINE
GRANDE ARRIVÉE DES COQUILLAGES
ALL THE REST OF PARIS
WRITING A STORY
"THE BEVERLY BOYS"
THE WELLCOME HOTEL
ROOM 26
IN 1955
IT'S FINISHED!
JANICE SAYS "I'M HUNGRY. ARE YOU?"
NIGHT
WE GO OUT
BEAUTIFUL STARS

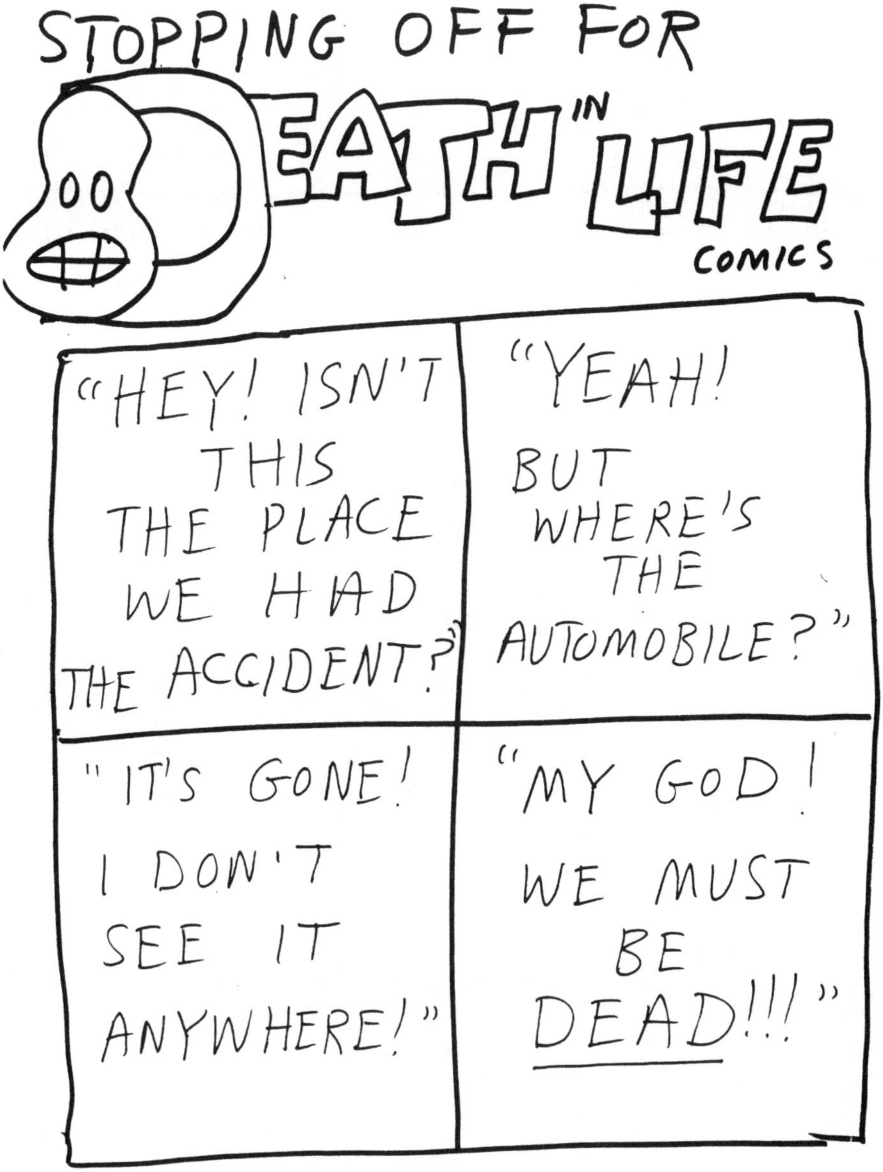
STOPPING OFF FOR
DEATH IN LIFE
COMICS
"HEY! ISN'T THIS THE PLACE WE HAD THE ACCIDENT?"
"YEAH! BUT WHERE'S THE AUTOMOBILE?"
"IT'S GONE! I DON'T SEE IT ANYWHERE!"
"MY GOD! WE MUST BE DEAD!!!"

MAKING CIGARS IN CUBA COMICS

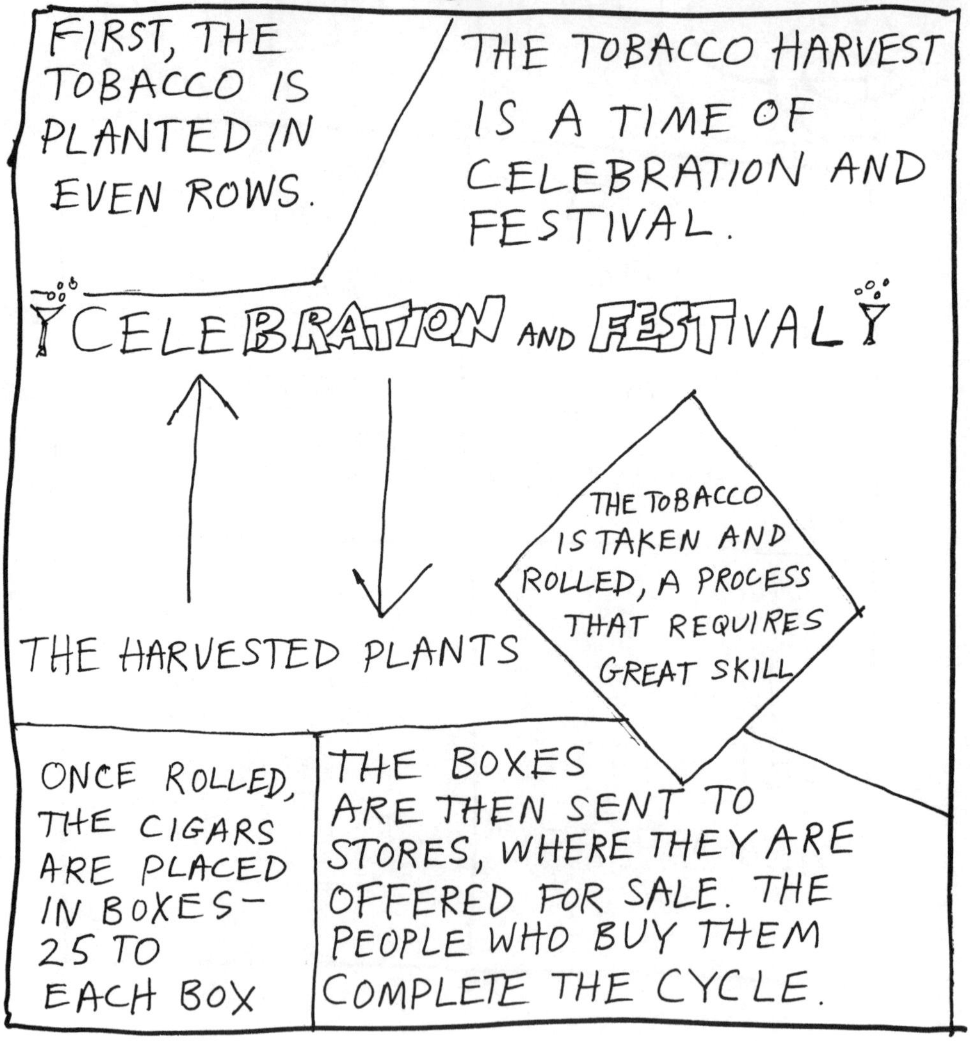

FIRST, THE TOBACCO IS PLANTED IN EVEN ROWS.
THE TOBACCO HARVEST IS A TIME OF CELEBRATION AND FESTIVAL.
CELEBRATION AND FESTIVAL
THE HARVESTED PLANTS
THE TOBACCO IS TAKEN AND ROLLED, A PROCESS THAT REQUIRES GREAT SKILL
ONCE ROLLED, THE CIGARS ARE PLACED IN BOXES- 25 TO EACH BOX
THE BOXES ARE THEN SENT TO STORES, WHERE THEY ARE OFFERED FOR SALE. THE PEOPLE WHO BUY THEM COMPLETE THE CYCLE.

BLANK COMICS

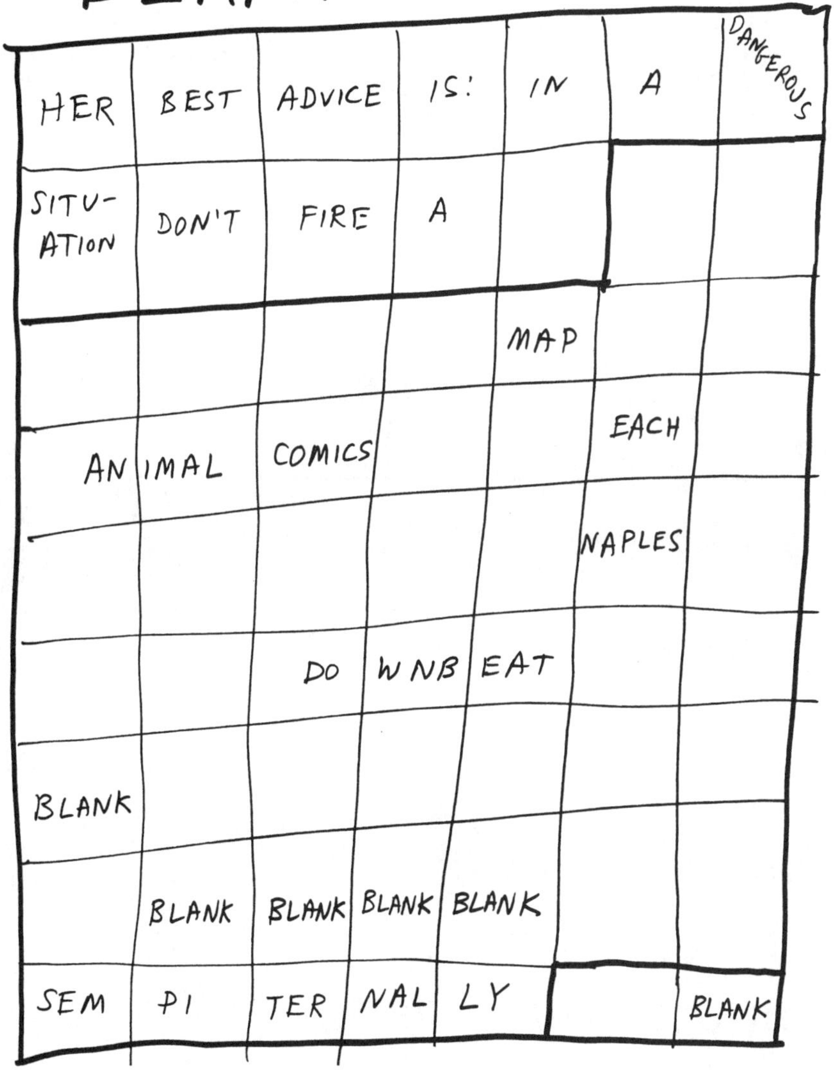

HER	BEST	ADVICE	IS:	IN	A	DANGEROUS
SITU-ATION	DON'T	FIRE	A			
				MAP		
AN IMAL	COMICS			EACH		
				NAPLES		
		DO	WNB	EAT		
BLANK						
	BLANK	BLANK	BLANK	BLANK		
SEM	PI	TER	NAL	LY		BLANK

BRER COMICS

A FAMILY GOES TO DISNEY-LAND	THEY GO ON "RIDES"	"LES GET SUMMEEN TO EAT!" "OKAY!
THEY GO INTO A HORSESHOE SHAPED RESTAURANT	AND SIT DOWN AT A BIG ROUND TABLE	THERE IS AN EMPTY SEAT NEXT TO ELLA, THE WIFE
ELLA IS VERY PRETTY	BRER FOX ENTERS THE RESTAURANT	HE GOES AND SITS DOWN NEXT TO ELLA
HE PUTS HIS RIGHT ARM AROUND HER SHOULDERS	ELLA TURNS AND LOOKS AT HIM, SURPRISED	BRER FOX STARES STRAIGHT AHEAD AND KEEPS HIS ARM AROUND ELLA'S SHOULDERS

BEAUTIFUL ELLA
BEAUTIFUL ELLA
BEAUTIFUL ELLA
BEAUTIFUL ELLA
BRER FOX
BEAUTIFUL ELLA
BEAUTIFUL ELLA
BEAUTIFUL ELLA
BRER FOX
*J*A*C*K*P*O*T*

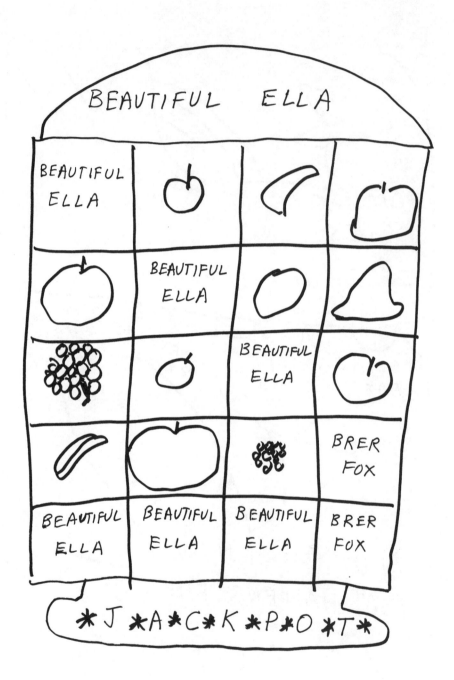

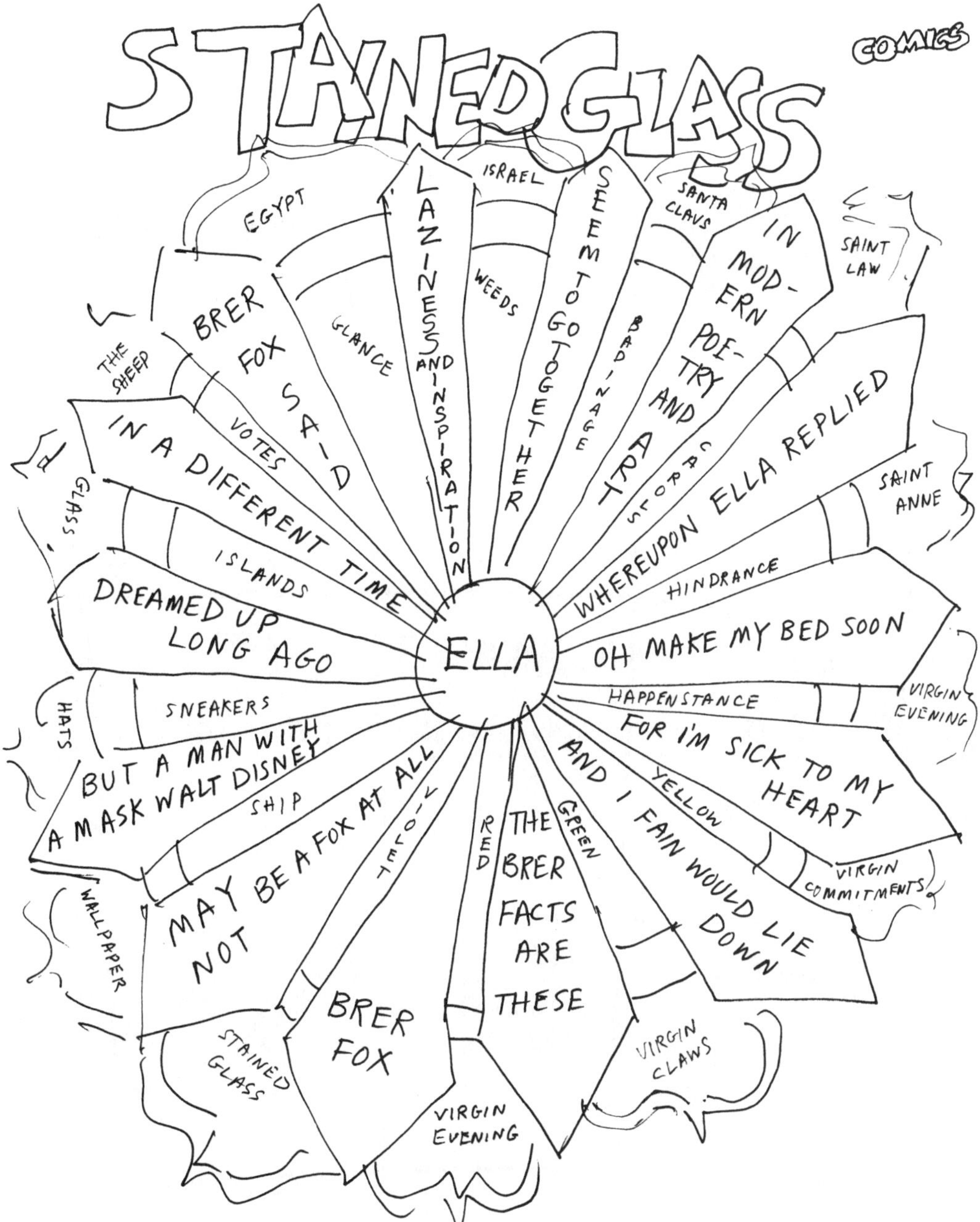
STAINED GLASS
COMICS
EGYPT
ISRAEL
SANTA CLAUS
SAINT LAW
LAZINESS AND INSPIRATION
SEEM TO GO TOGETHER
IN MODERN POETRY AND ART
WEEDS
GLANCE
BADINAGE
BRER FOX SAID
THE SHEEP
VOTES
IN A DIFFERENT TIME
GLASS
ISLANDS
WHEREUPON ELLA REPLIED
SAINT ANNE
HINDRANCE
DREAMED UP LONG AGO
ELLA
OH MAKE MY BED SOON
HAPPENSTANCE
VIRGIN EVENING
HATS
SNEAKERS
BUT A MAN WITH A MASK WALT DISNEY
SHIP
FOR I'M SICK TO MY HEART
YELLOW
VIRGIN COMMITMENTS
AND I FAIN WOULD LIE DOWN
GREEN
RED
THE BRER FACTS ARE THESE
MAY BE A FOX AT ALL NOT
WALLPAPER
BRER FOX
STAINED GLASS
VIRGIN EVENING
VIRGIN CLAWS

BRER COMICS

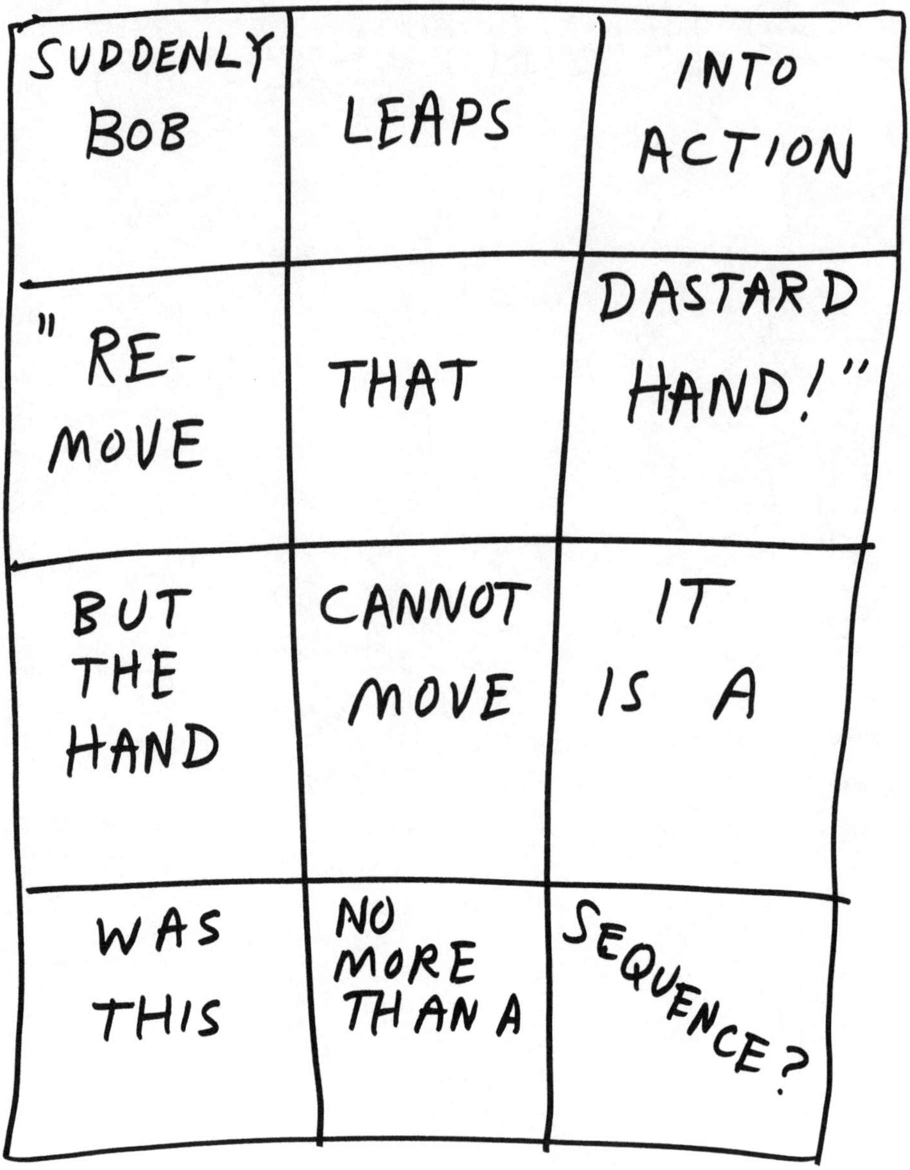

SUDDENLY BOB	LEAPS	INTO ACTION
" RE-MOVE	THAT	DASTARD HAND!"
BUT THE HAND	CANNOT MOVE	IT IS A
WAS THIS	NO MORE THAN A	SEQUENCE?

BRER COMICS

FINALLY BOB SAID, "BRER
FOX, I AM BEFUDDLED. BUT
YOU HAVE NOT WON ELLA'S
HEART JUST BY STARING AHEAD."

BRER COMICS

BRER FOX TELLS US THE STORY OF HIS LIFE	"HOW DID YOU COME TO LOVE A HUMAN GIRL?" ONE ASKED	"I WAS BORN AMIDST FOREIGN RABBITS," BRER FOX SAID
WE IMAGINED THE OLD SILK TRAIL, SAMARKAND-KUNMING	"NO." BRER FOX CORRECTED US— "NOT THERE.	I WAS BRED AMONG FOREIGN HABITS," HE SAID
A SMILE UTTERED ITS WISDOM ON HIS FACE	O BRER HEAD O BRER HEAD! ELLA WAS MOVED	"A RABBIT WAS MY MASTER," BRER FOX SAID
"THEN I FELL INTO THE WORLD OF DISNEY, WHERE MINNIE MOUSE LIVES—	'OF INDEPENDENT MEANS, AND ... [OWNING] A SMALL HOUSE IN THE MIDST OF UNATTRACTIVE SCENERY, WHERE, WITH NO SERVANT AND LITTLE FURNITURE, SHE BUSIES HERSELF ABOUT TRIFLES UNTIL MICKEY COMES.'" HE WEPT.	

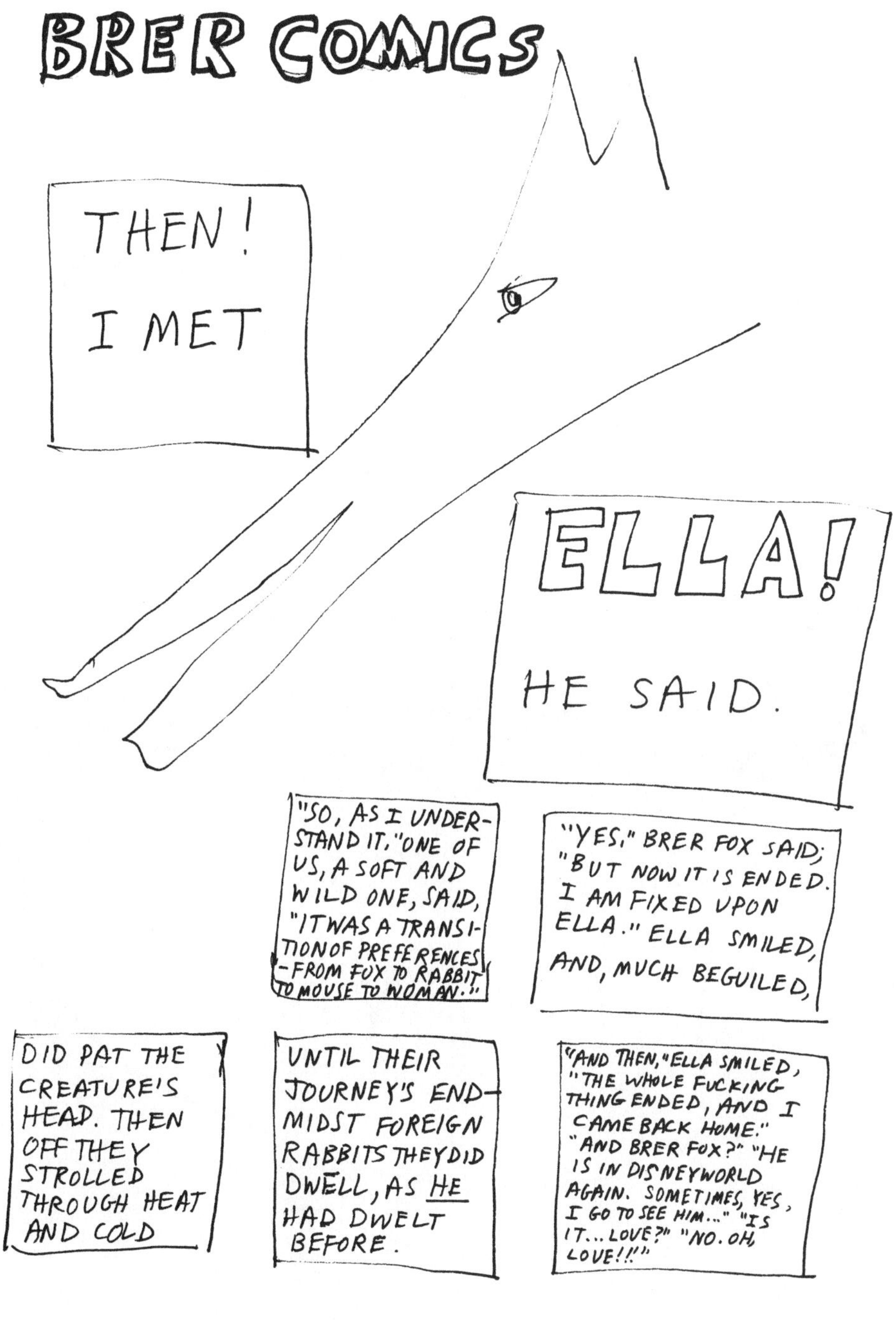
BRER COMICS
THEN! I MET
ELLA! HE SAID.
"SO, AS I UNDERSTAND IT," ONE OF US, A SOFT AND WILD ONE, SAID, "IT WAS A TRANSITION OF PREFERENCES - FROM FOX TO RABBIT TO MOUSE TO WOMAN."
"YES," BRER FOX SAID; "BUT NOW IT IS ENDED. I AM FIXED UPON ELLA." ELLA SMILED, AND, MUCH BEGUILED,
DID PAT THE CREATURE'S HEAD. THEN OFF THEY STROLLED THROUGH HEAT AND COLD
UNTIL THEIR JOURNEY'S END- MIDST FOREIGN RABBITS THEY DID DWELL, AS HE HAD DWELT BEFORE.
"AND THEN," ELLA SMILED, "THE WHOLE FUCKING THING ENDED, AND I CAME BACK HOME." "AND BRER FOX?" "HE IS IN DISNEYWORLD AGAIN. SOMETIMES, YES, I GO TO SEE HIM..." "IS IT... LOVE?" "NO. OH, LOVE!!"

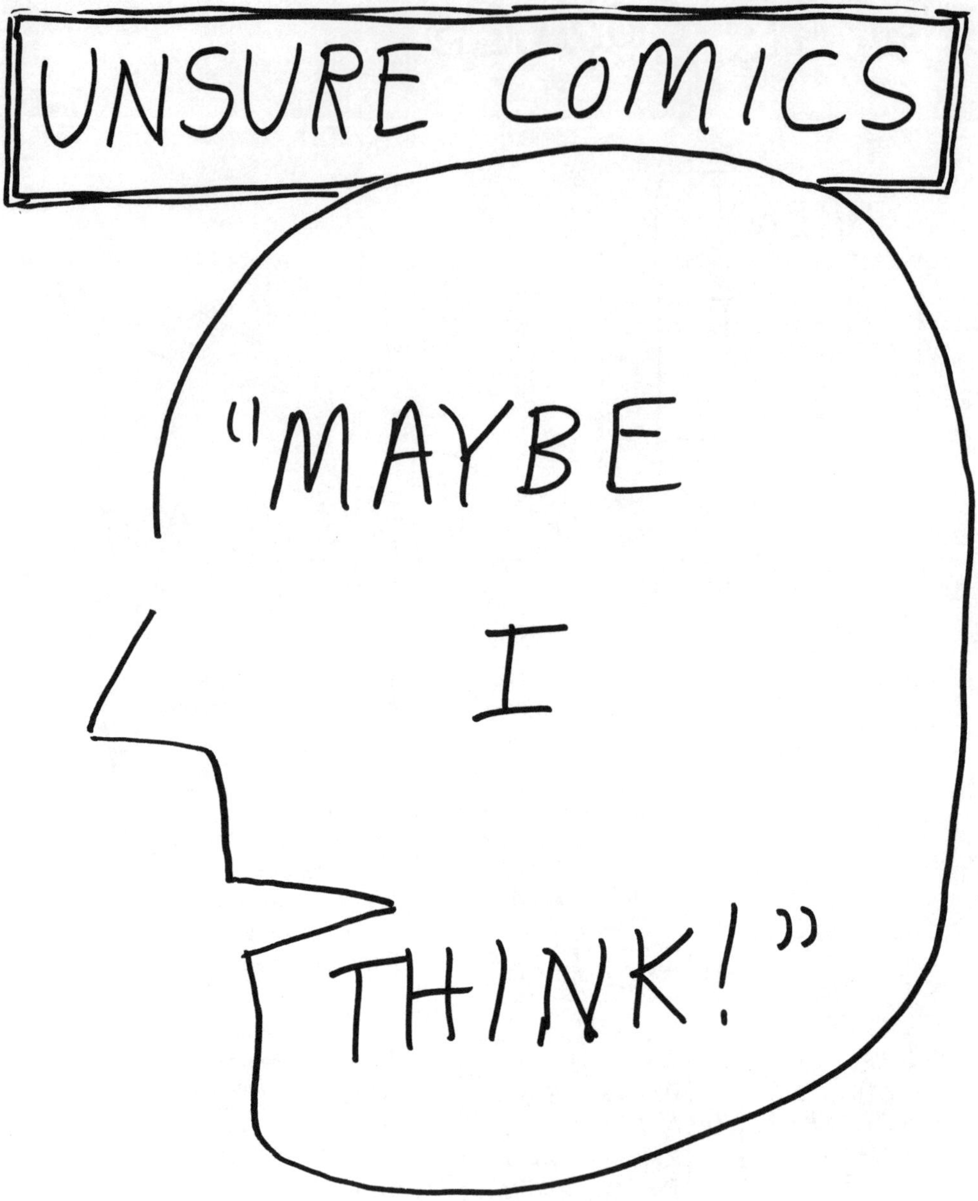
UNSURE COMICS
"MAYBE I THINK!"

SUBWAY COMICS

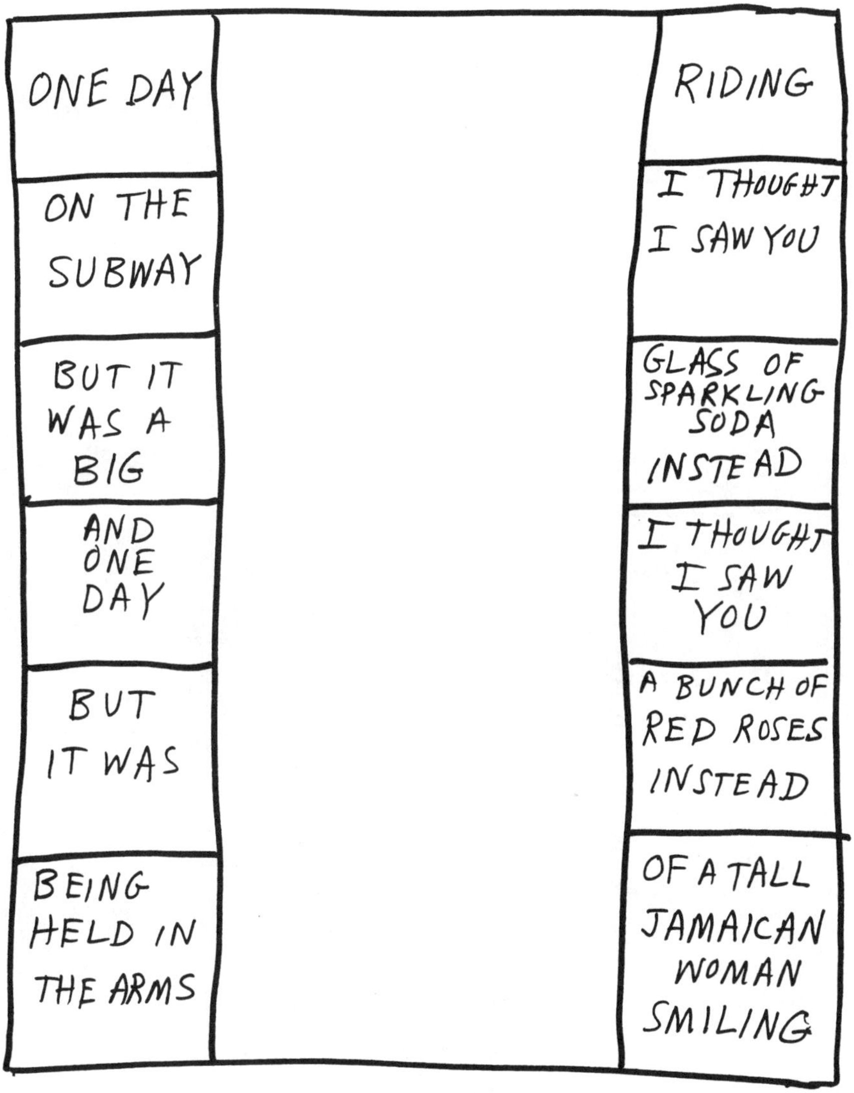

ONE DAY		RIDING
ON THE SUBWAY		I THOUGHT I SAW YOU
BUT IT WAS A BIG		GLASS OF SPARKLING SODA INSTEAD
AND ONE DAY		I THOUGHT I SAW YOU
BUT IT WAS		A BUNCH OF RED ROSES INSTEAD
BEING HELD IN THE ARMS		OF A TALL JAMAICAN WOMAN SMILING

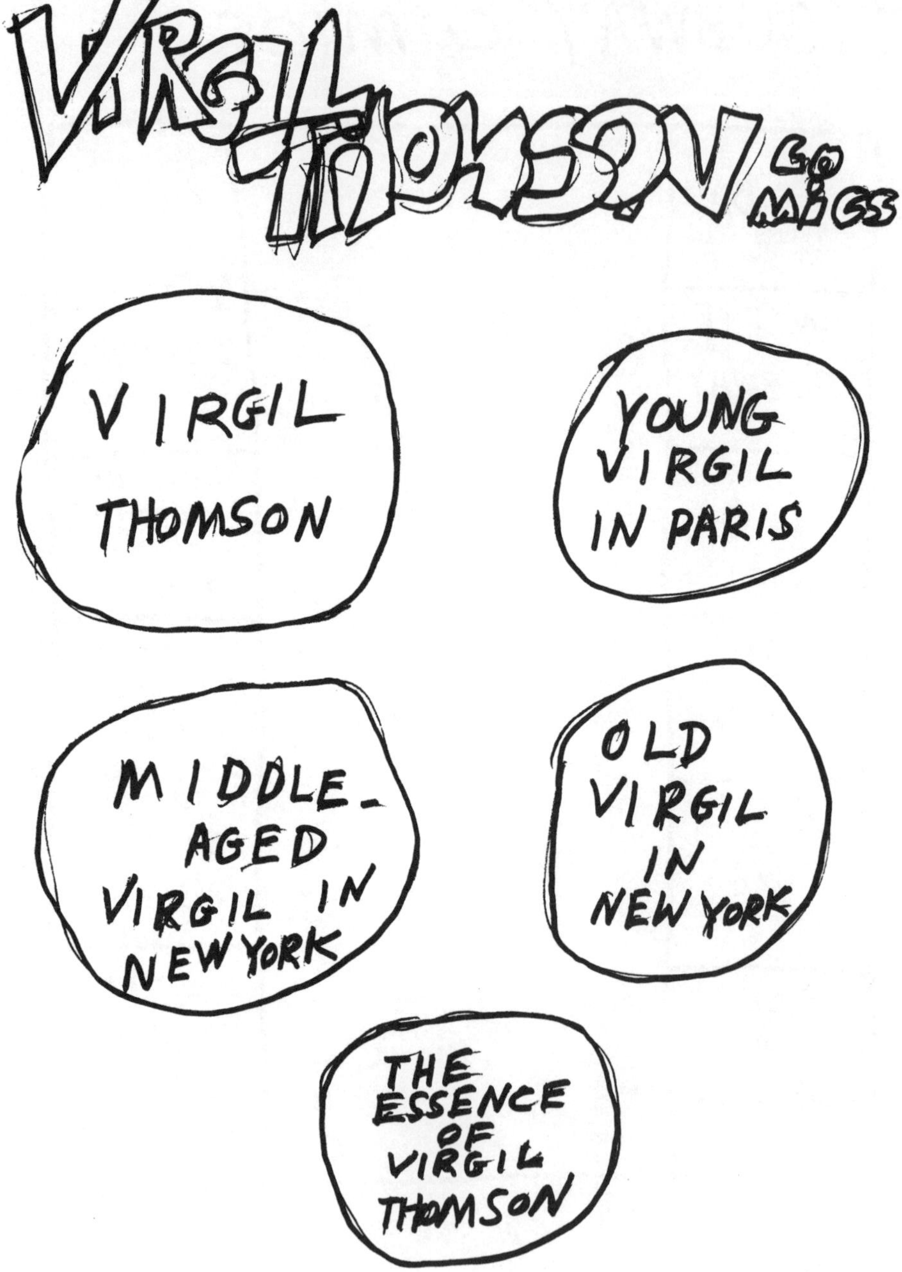
VIRGIL THOMSON COMICS
VIRGIL THOMSON
YOUNG VIRGIL IN PARIS
MIDDLE-AGED VIRGIL IN NEW YORK
OLD VIRGIL IN NEW YORK
THE ESSENCE OF VIRGIL THOMSON

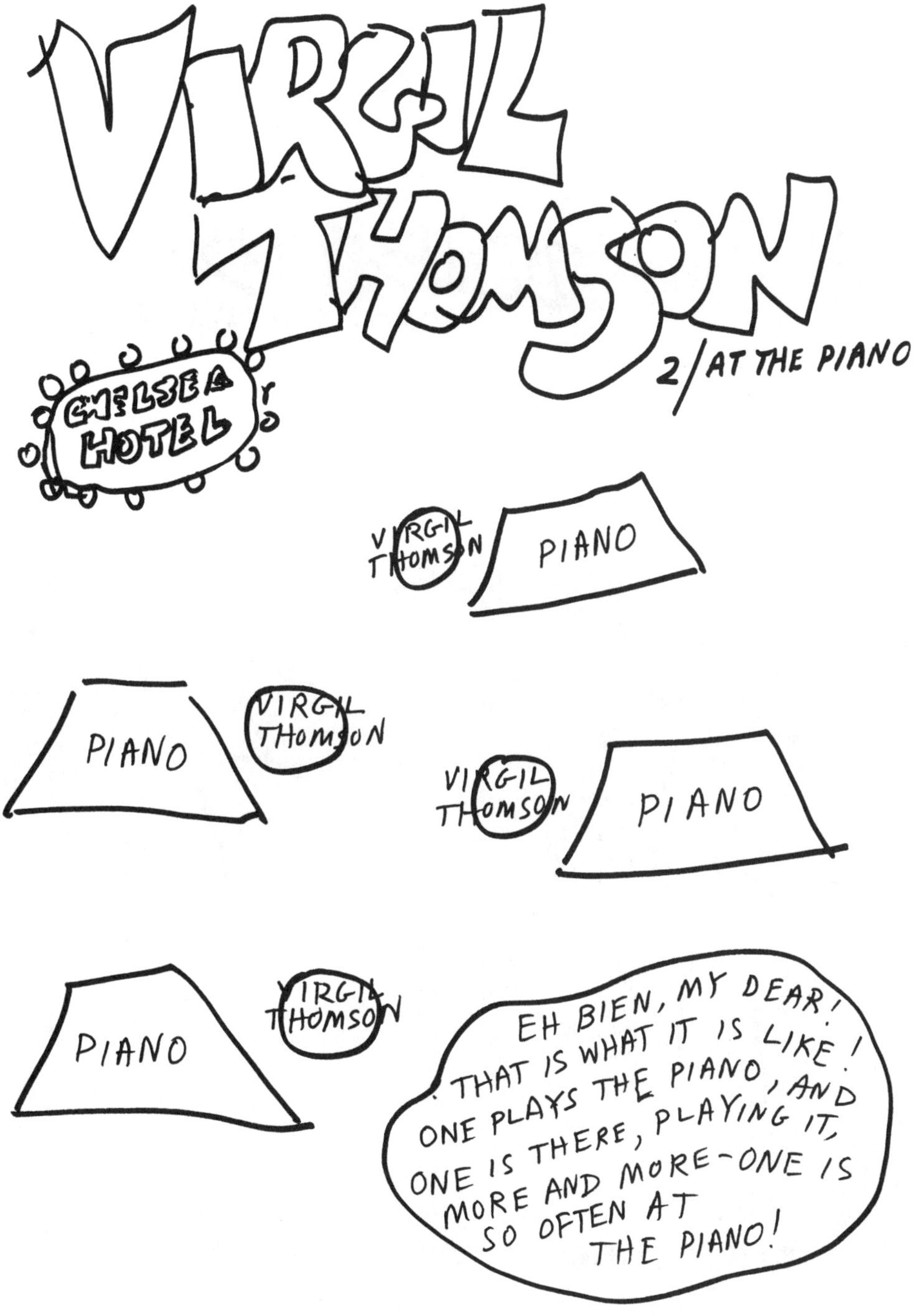
VIRGIL THOMSON
2/AT THE PIANO
CHELSEA HOTEL
VIRGIL THOMSON
PIANO
PIANO
VIRGIL THOMSON
VIRGIL THOMSON
PIANO
PIANO
VIRGIL THOMSON
EH BIEN, MY DEAR! THAT IS WHAT IT IS LIKE! THAT IS WHAT IT IS LIKE! ONE PLAYS THE PIANO, AND ONE IS THERE, PLAYING IT, MORE AND MORE-ONE IS SO OFTEN AT THE PIANO!

VIRGIL THOMSON

...... AND HIS FRIENDS

VTC 3

✱ SEE IDENTIFICATION KEY ON NEXT PAGE

KEY:

NAME	FRUIT FLOWER OR VEGETABLE	BIRD OR ANIMAL
1 — JOHN CAGE	APPLE	FOX
2 — J GORDON LIDDY	LEMON	WOLF
3 — MILES DAVIS	PLUM	DOG
4 — ABE LINCOLN	CHERRY	CAT
5 — TWIGGY	TWIG	MOUSE
6 — REINHOLD NEIBUHR	ORANGE	MONKEY
7 — OSCAR LEVANT	BANANA	APE
8 — ED KRANEPOOL	CIGAR	HEDGEHOG
9 — DR. CALIGARI	EGGPLANT	FERRET
10 — LINCOLN KIRSTEN	CORN ON THE COB	ELEPHANT
11 — LILLIAN HELLMAN	FIG	LYNX
12 — JACOB RUPERT	DANDELION	HIPPOPOTAMUS
13 — HENRY GREEN	HONEYDEW MELON	JACKAL

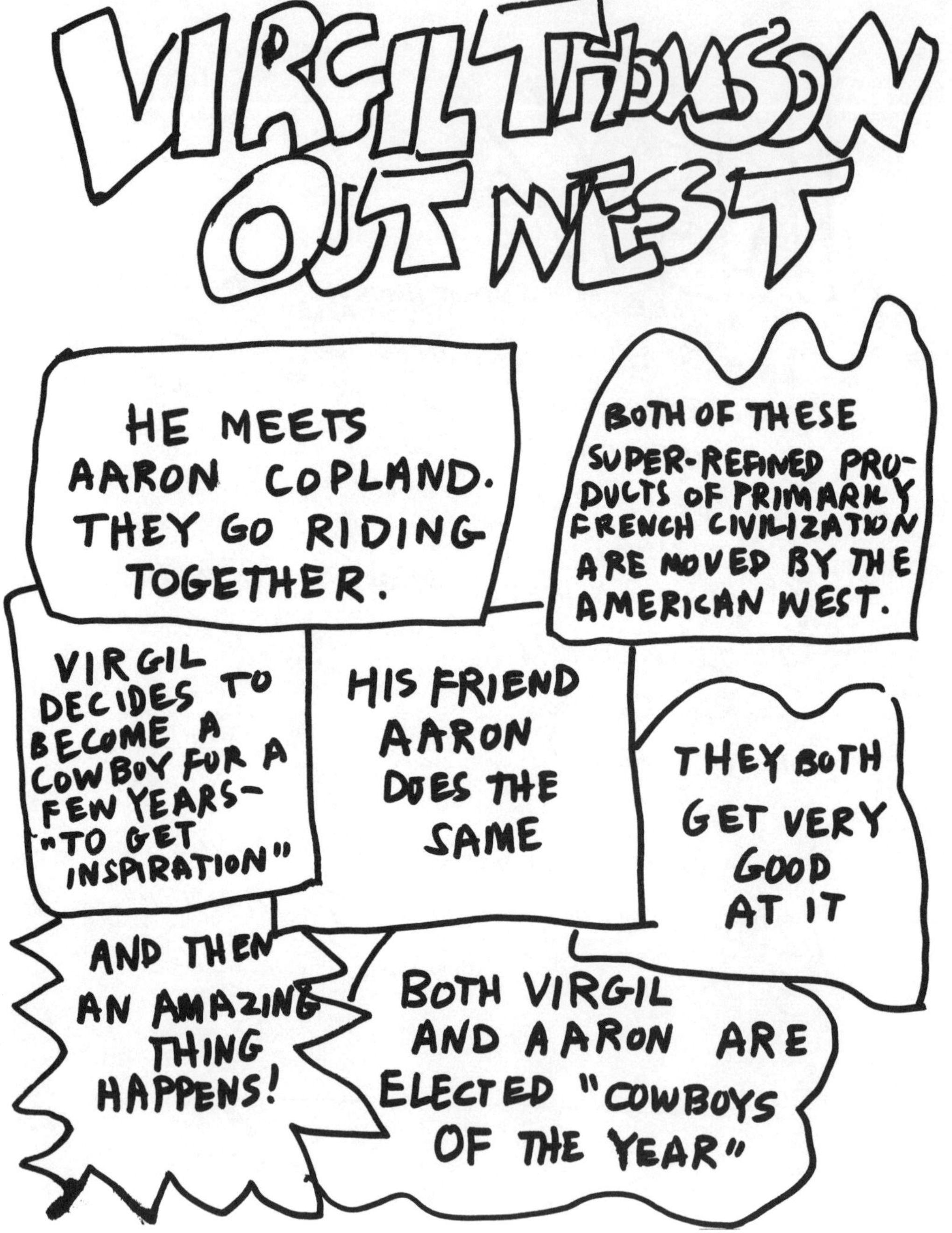
VIRGIL THOMSON OUT WEST
HE MEETS AARON COPLAND. THEY GO RIDING TOGETHER.
BOTH OF THESE SUPER-REFINED PRODUCTS OF PRIMARILY FRENCH CIVILIZATION ARE MOVED BY THE AMERICAN WEST.
VIRGIL DECIDES TO BECOME A COWBOY FOR A FEW YEARS- "TO GET INSPIRATION"
HIS FRIEND AARON DOES THE SAME
THEY BOTH GET VERY GOOD AT IT
AND THEN AN AMAZING THING HAPPENS!
BOTH VIRGIL AND AARON ARE ELECTED "COWBOYS OF THE YEAR"

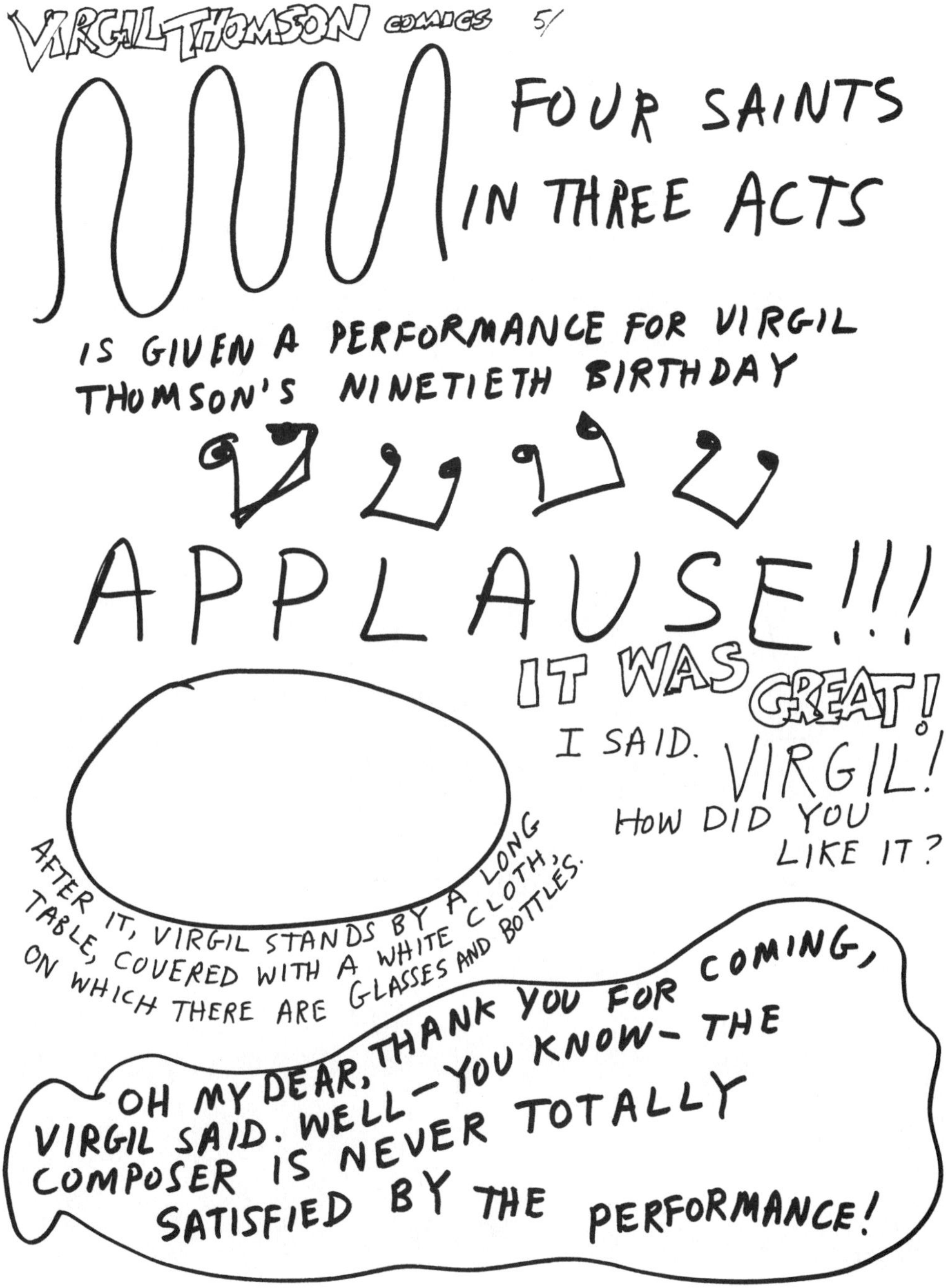
VIRGIL THOMSON COMICS 5/
FOUR SAINTS IN THREE ACTS
IS GIVEN A PERFORMANCE FOR VIRGIL THOMSON'S NINETIETH BIRTHDAY
APPLAUSE!!!
IT WAS GREAT!
I SAID. VIRGIL!
HOW DID YOU LIKE IT?
AFTER IT, VIRGIL STANDS BY A LONG TABLE, COVERED WITH A WHITE CLOTH, ON WHICH THERE ARE GLASSES AND BOTTLES.
OH MY DEAR, THANK YOU FOR COMING, VIRGIL SAID. WELL-YOU KNOW- THE COMPOSER IS NEVER TOTALLY SATISFIED BY THE PERFORMANCE!

CIVILIZATION

... AND ITS DISCONTENTS

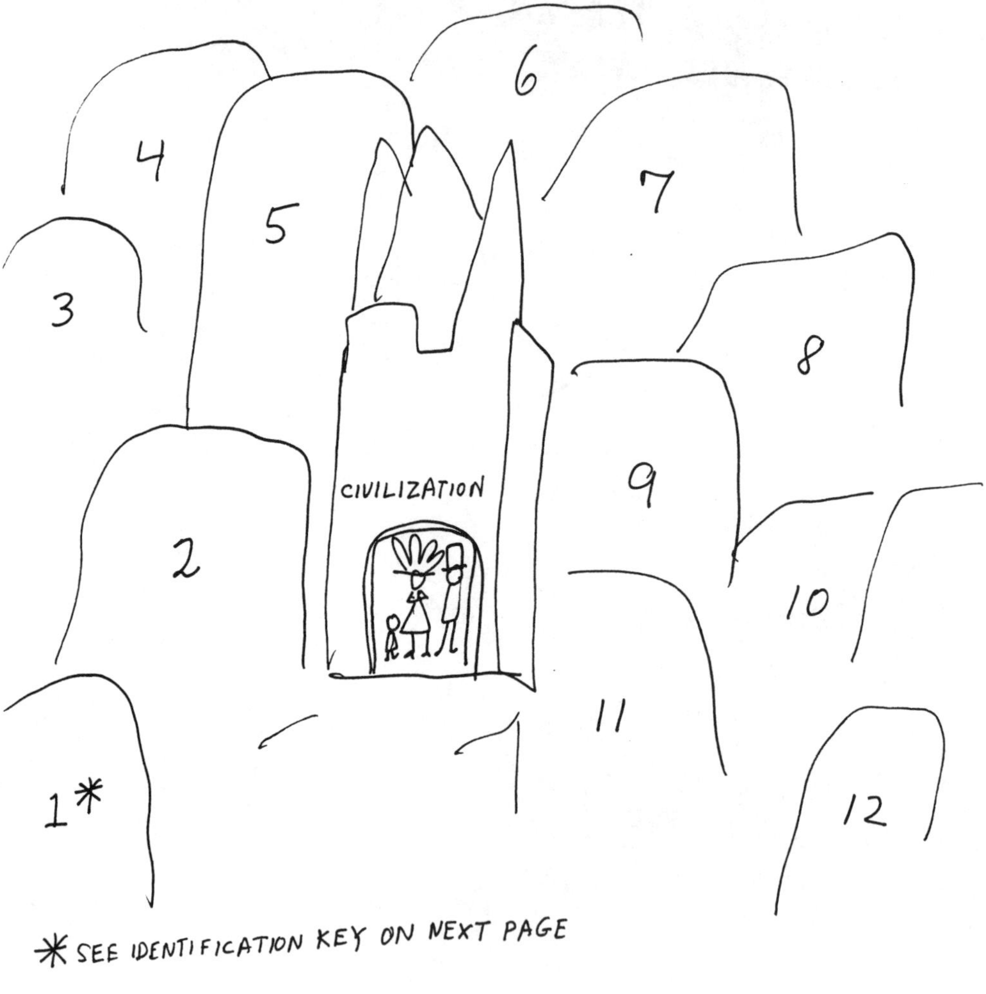

6
4
5
7
3
8
CIVILIZATION
9
2
10
11
1*
12

* SEE IDENTIFICATION KEY ON NEXT PAGE

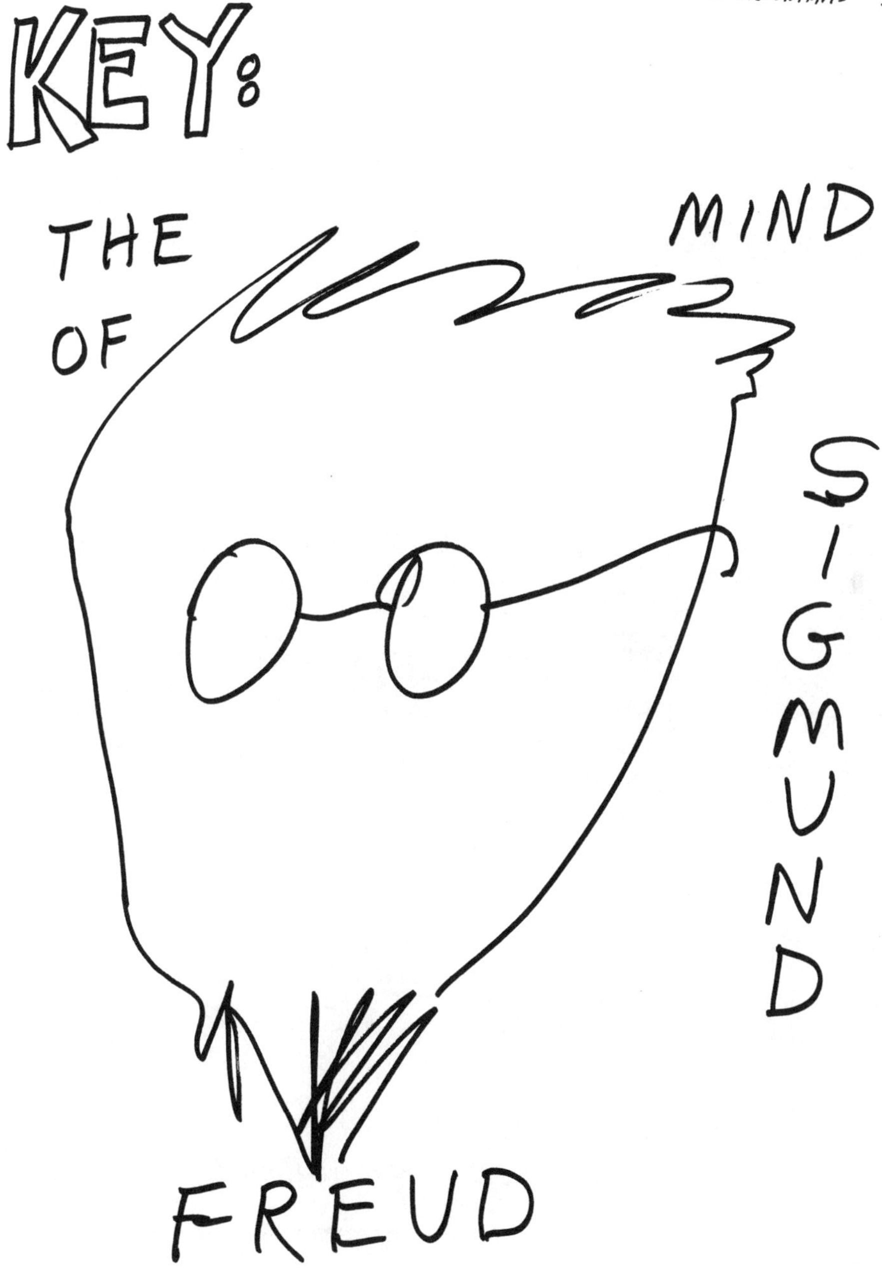
KEY:
THE MIND OF SIGMUND FREUD

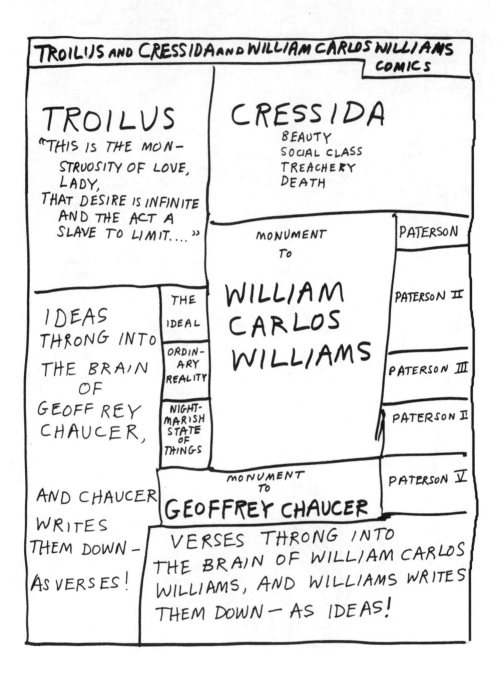

TROILUS AND CRESSIDA AND WILLIAM CARLOS WILLIAMS COMICS

TROILUS
"THIS IS THE MON-
STRUOSITY OF LOVE,
LADY,
THAT DESIRE IS INFINITE
AND THE ACT A
SLAVE TO LIMIT...."

CRESSIDA
BEAUTY
SOCIAL CLASS
TREACHERY
DEATH

MONUMENT
TO
WILLIAM
CARLOS
WILLIAMS

PATERSON

PATERSON II

PATERSON III

PATERSON II

PATERSON II

IDEAS
THRONG INTO
THE BRAIN
OF
GEOFFREY
CHAUCER,

THE
IDEAL

ORDIN-
ARY
REALITY

NIGHT-
MARISH
STATE
OF
THINGS

MONUMENT
TO
GEOFFREY CHAUCER

PATERSON V

AND CHAUCER
WRITES
THEM DOWN —
AS VERSES!

VERSES THRONG INTO
THE BRAIN OF WILLIAM CARLOS
WILLIAMS, AND WILLIAMS WRITES
THEM DOWN — AS IDEAS!

84

HONORÉ DE COMICS

BALZAC

EUGÉNIE GRANDIN

"IN YOUTH IS PLEASURE"

LOST ILLUSIONS

DIES OF A

REAL NAME: MUNIPOLE STRAVONSKI

FATHER GORIOT

HORROR VACUI

HEART ATTACK

COUSIN PONS

"IT WAS WORTH IT!"

THE LILY IN THE VALLEY

"I AM DEAD!"

A TENEBROUS AFFAIR

FROM DRINKING COFFEE ALL NIGHT LONG

"I HAVE TO ACHIEVE!"

COUSIN BETTY

"NOW WE KNOW!"

FLAGS OF DIFFERENT NATIONS

THAILAND

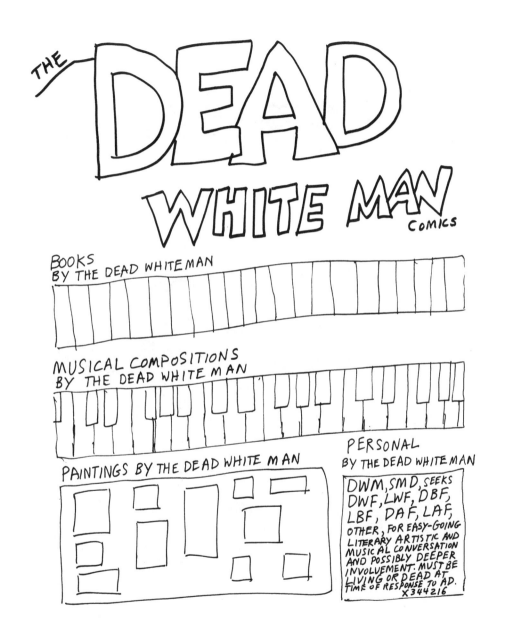

THE DEAD WHITE MAN COMICS

BOOKS
BY THE DEAD WHITE MAN

MUSICAL COMPOSITIONS
BY THE DEAD WHITE MAN

PAINTINGS BY THE DEAD WHITE MAN

PERSONAL
BY THE DEAD WHITE MAN

DWM, SMD, SEEKS DWF, LWF, DBF, LBF, DAF, LAF, OTHER, FOR EASY-GOING LITERARY, ARTISTIC AND MUSICAL CONVERSATION AND POSSIBLY DEEPER INVOLVEMENT. MUST BE LIVING OR DEAD AT TIME OF RESPONSE TO AD.
X344216

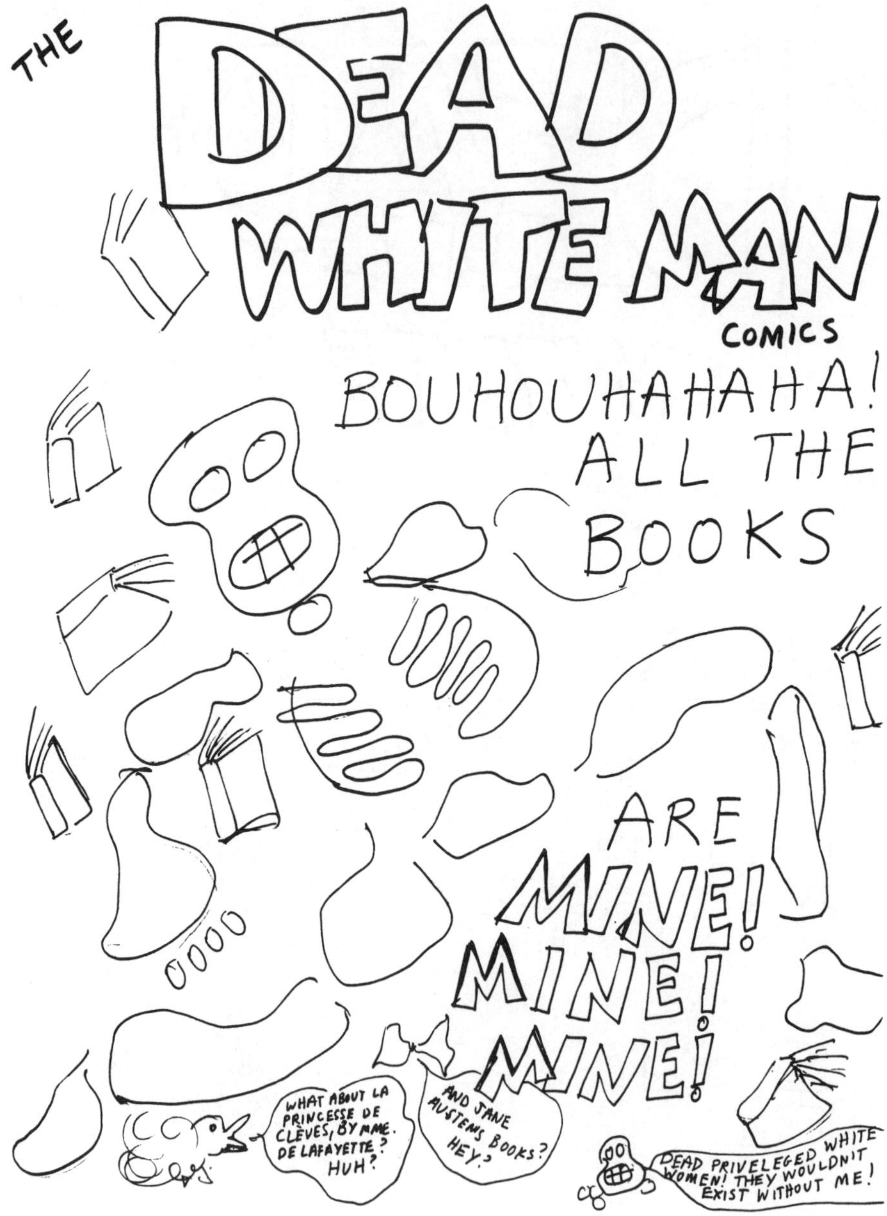
THE
DEAD WHITE MAN
COMICS
BOUHOUHAHAHA! ALL THE BOOKS
ARE MINE! MINE! MINE!
WHAT ABOUT LA PRINCESSE DE CLÈVES, BY MME. DE LAFAYETTE? HUH?
AND JANE AUSTENS BOOKS? HEY?
DEAD PRIVELEGED WHITE WOMEN! THEY WOULDNIT EXIST WITHOUT ME!

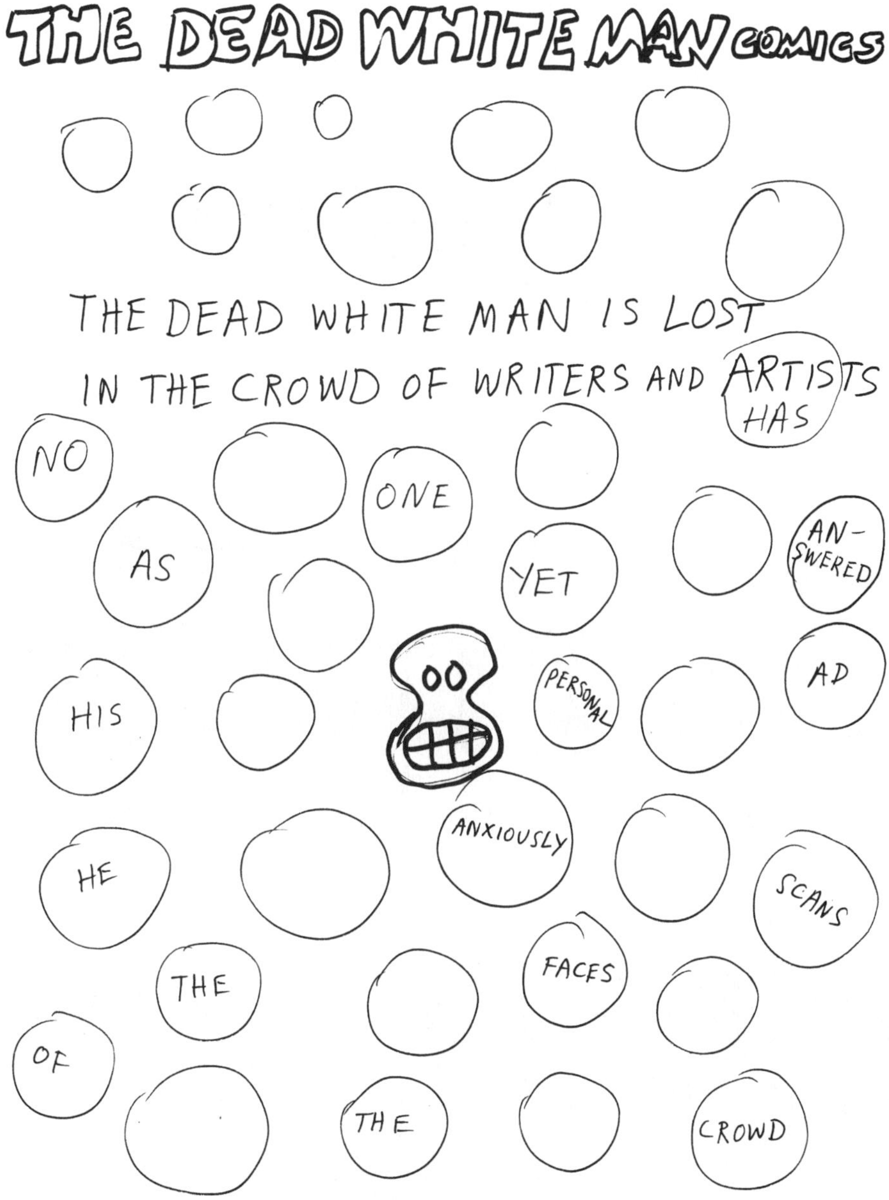

THE DEAD WHITE MAN COMICS
THE DEAD WHITE MAN IS LOST
IN THE CROWD OF WRITERS AND ARTISTS
HAS
NO
ONE
AS
YET
AN-SWERED
HIS
PERSONAL
AD
HE
ANXIOUSLY
SCANS
THE
FACES
OF
THE
CROWD

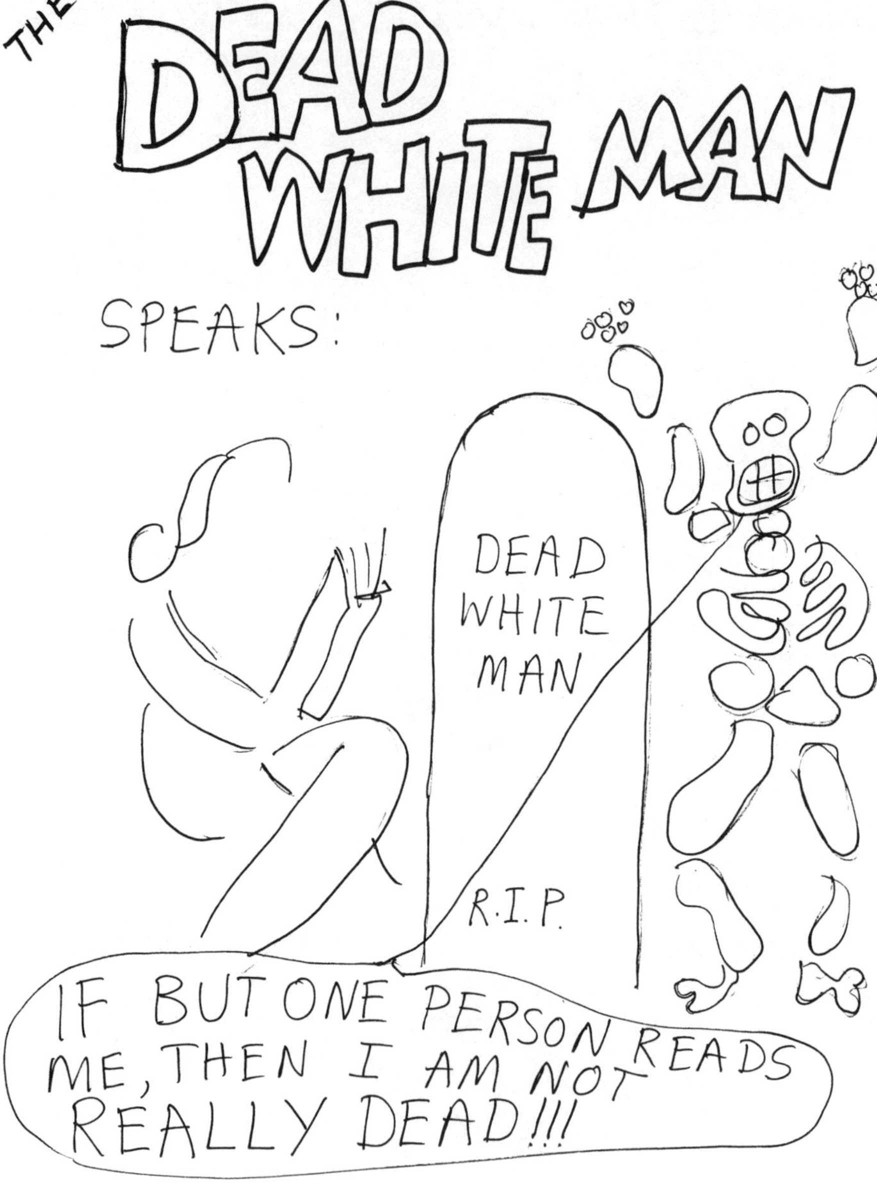
THE DEAD WHITE MAN
SPEAKS:
DEAD WHITE MAN
R.I.P.
IF BUT ONE PERSON READS ME, THEN I AM NOT REALLY DEAD!!!

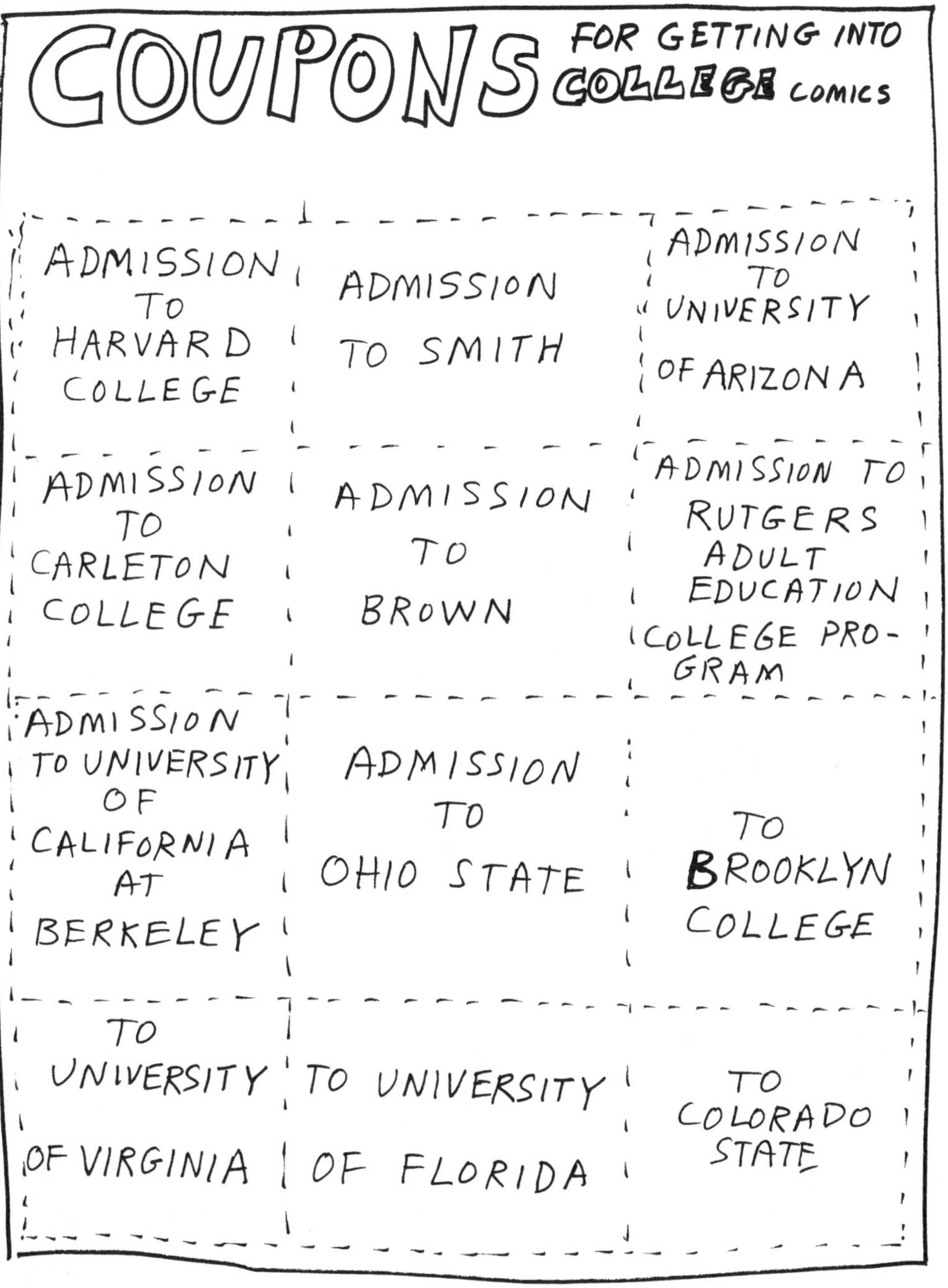

COUPONS

ADMISSION TO HARVARD COLLEGE	ADMISSION TO SMITH	ADMISSION TO UNIVERSITY OF ARIZONA
ADMISSION TO CARLETON COLLEGE	ADMISSION TO BROWN	ADMISSION TO RUTGERS ADULT EDUCATION COLLEGE PROGRAM
ADMISSION TO UNIVERSITY OF CALIFORNIA AT BERKELEY	ADMISSION TO OHIO STATE	TO BROOKLYN COLLEGE
TO UNIVERSITY OF VIRGINIA	TO UNIVERSITY OF FLORIDA	TO COLORADO STATE

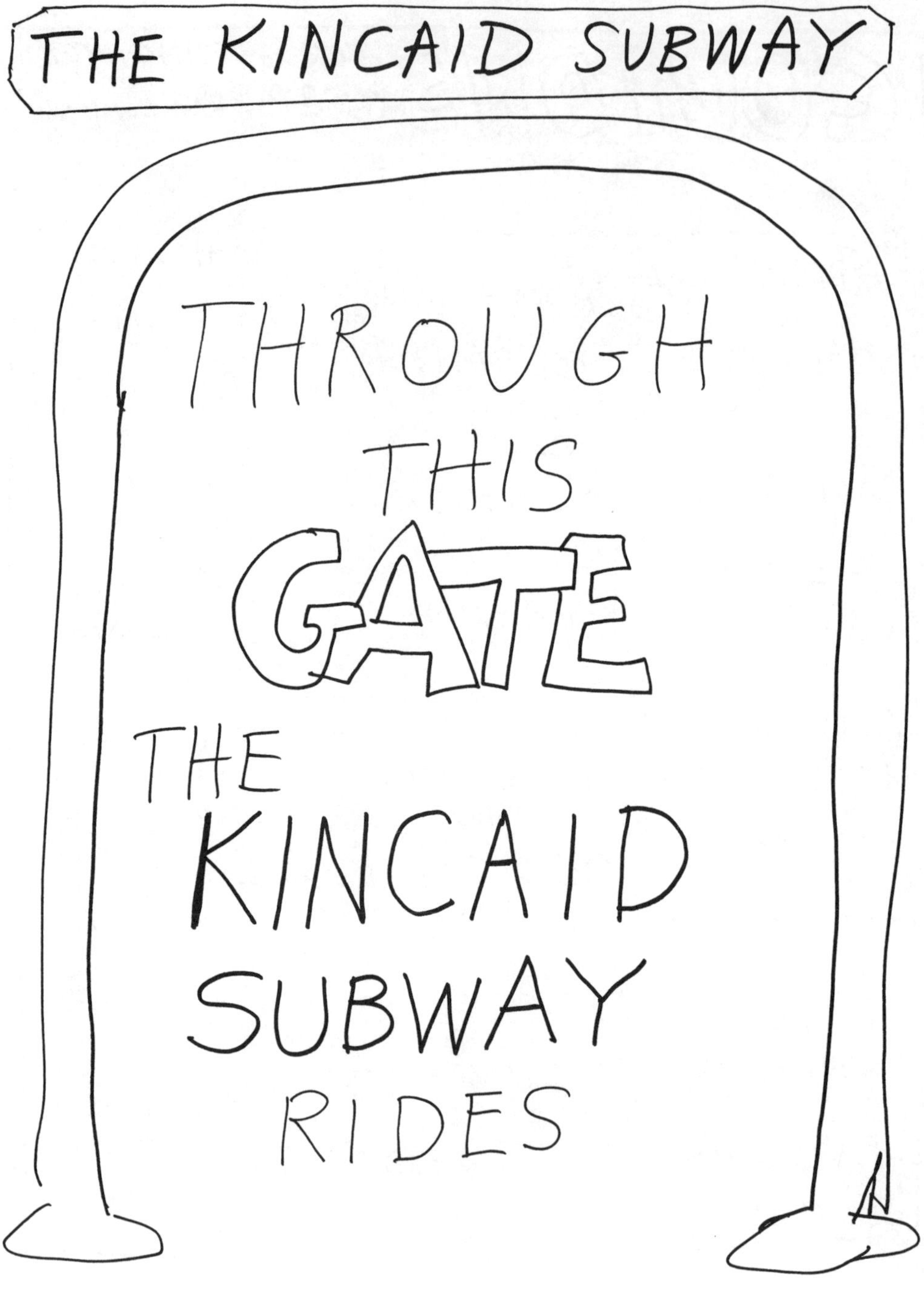
THE KINCAID SUBWAY
THROUGH THIS GATE THE KINCAID SUBWAY RIDES

THE KINCAID SUBWAY

GOOD	MORN-ING!	SANG THE	SWEDISH
SUB-STITUTE	AT LAST	THE	TITLE
OF DRINK-ING	WATER	IS WHEN	THE APPLE
FORM-LESSLY	CRYING	TODAY	KENNETH
SUNRISE	O ABOUT!	MOVE-MENT	SHIP-EASING RAGS!

THE KINCAID SUBWAY

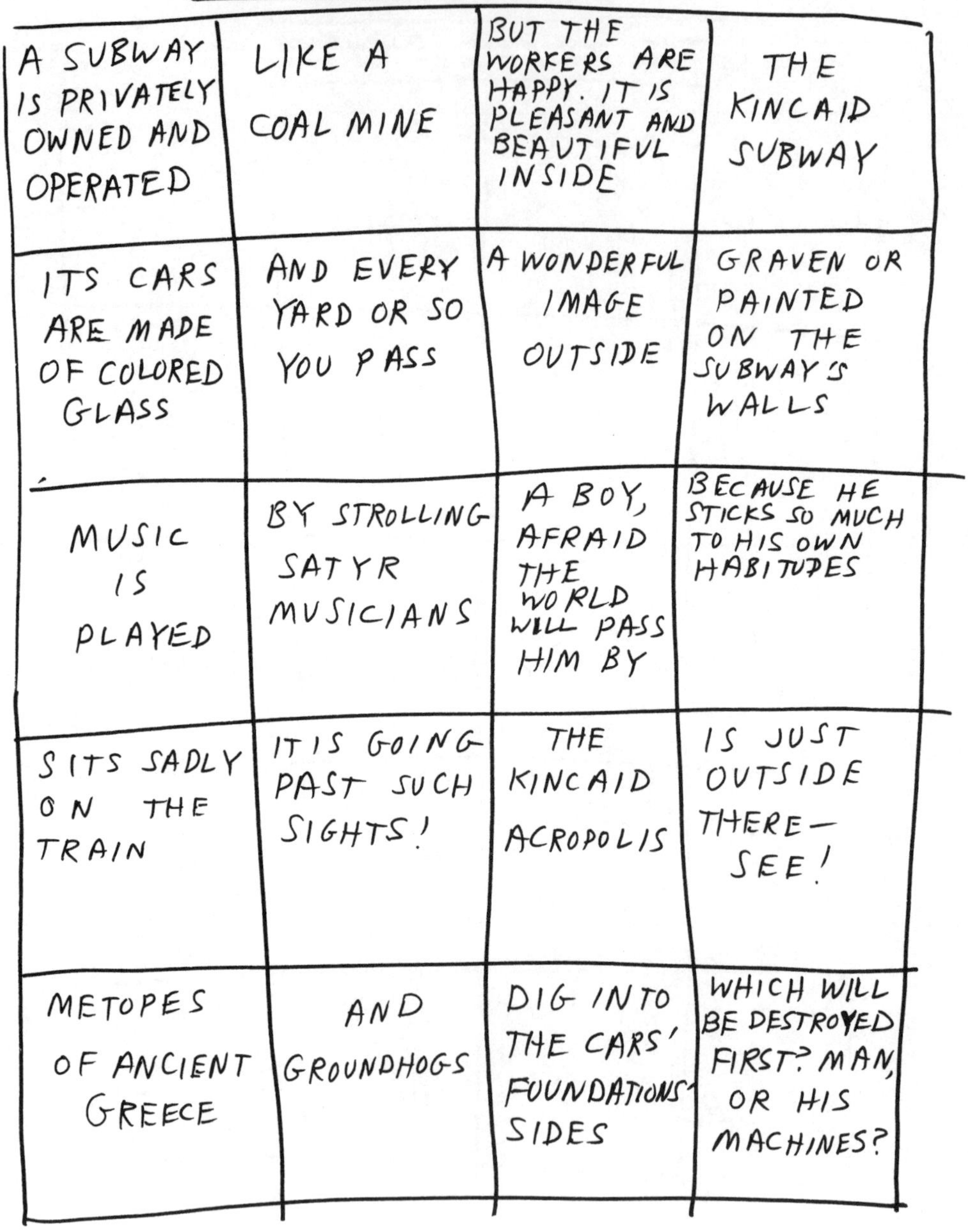

A SUBWAY IS PRIVATELY OWNED AND OPERATED	LIKE A COAL MINE	BUT THE WORKERS ARE HAPPY. IT IS PLEASANT AND BEAUTIFUL INSIDE	THE KINCAID SUBWAY
ITS CARS ARE MADE OF COLORED GLASS	AND EVERY YARD OR SO YOU PASS	A WONDERFUL IMAGE OUTSIDE	GRAVEN OR PAINTED ON THE SUBWAY'S WALLS
MUSIC IS PLAYED	BY STROLLING SATYR MUSICIANS	A BOY, AFRAID THE WORLD WILL PASS HIM BY	BECAUSE HE STICKS SO MUCH TO HIS OWN HABITUDES
SITS SADLY ON THE TRAIN	IT IS GOING PAST SUCH SIGHTS!	THE KINCAID ACROPOLIS	IS JUST OUTSIDE THERE— SEE!
METOPES OF ANCIENT GREECE	AND GROUNDHOGS	DIG INTO THE CARS' FOUNDATIONS' SIDES	WHICH WILL BE DESTROYED FIRST? MAN, OR HIS MACHINES?

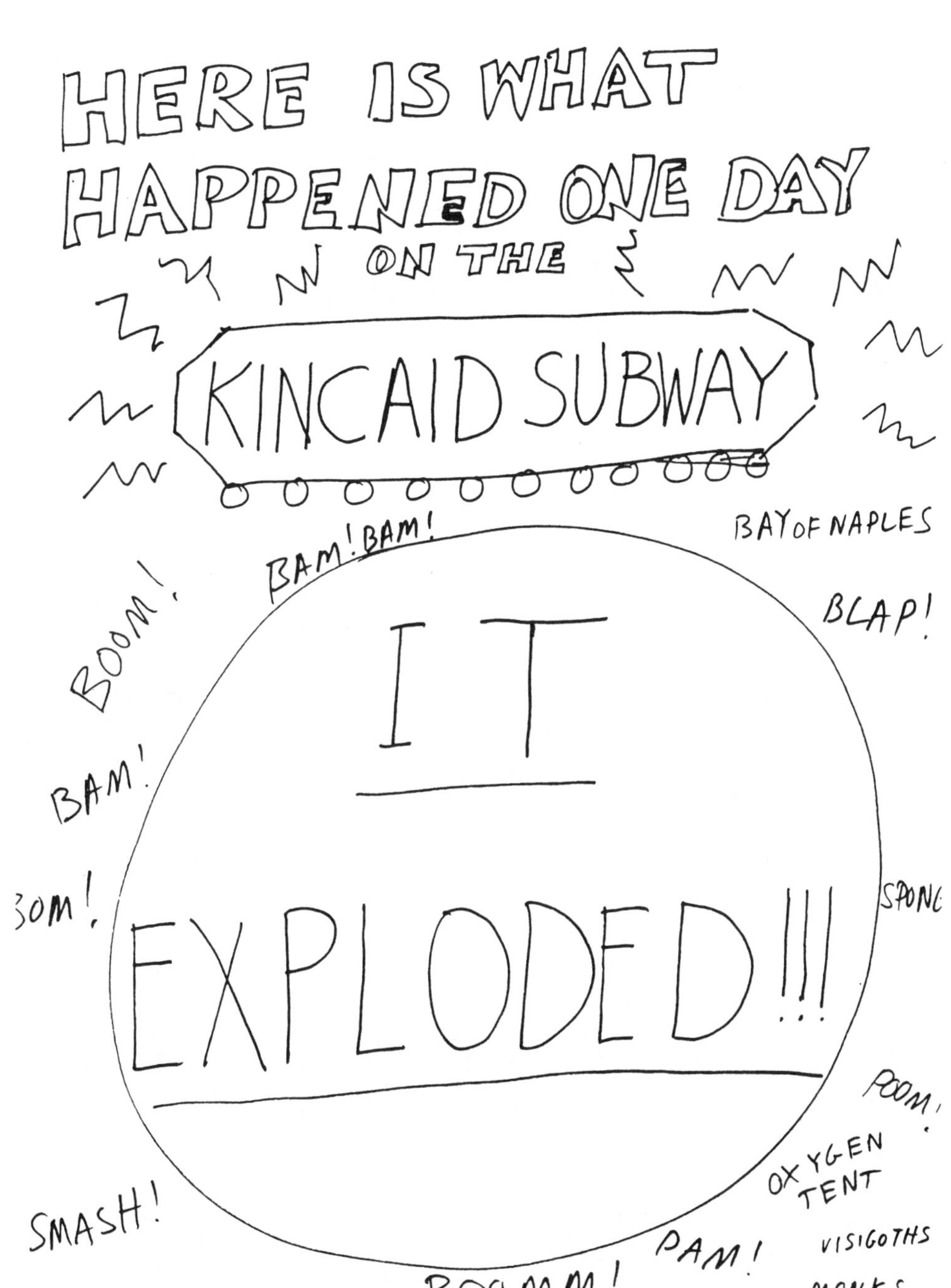
HERE IS WHAT HAPPENED ONE DAY
ON THE
KINCAID SUBWAY
BAM! BAM!
BAY OF NAPLES
BOOM!
BLAP!
IT
BAM!
30M!
SPONC
EXPLODED!!!
POOM!
OXYGEN TENT
SMASH!
PAM!
VISIGOTHS
BOOMM!
MONKS

THE KINCAID SUBWAY

THIS	IS A CRY	OF INSTINCTIVE	HAPPINESS
MAYBE	IT	WON'T	COLLAPSE
AFTER	ALL	A	GREAT
HEARKENING	TO NATURAL THINGS	PEACH TREES IN BLOSSOM	GIRLS DOGS
THANK YOU	THIS KINCAID SUBWAY AFTER ALL	FORGETS	THE SHADOWS OF LIFE

TO WHOM SHALL I ADDRESS THIS RIDE

ON THE KINCAID SUBWAY?

YOU'RE AMAZING

YOU'RE
AMAZING!

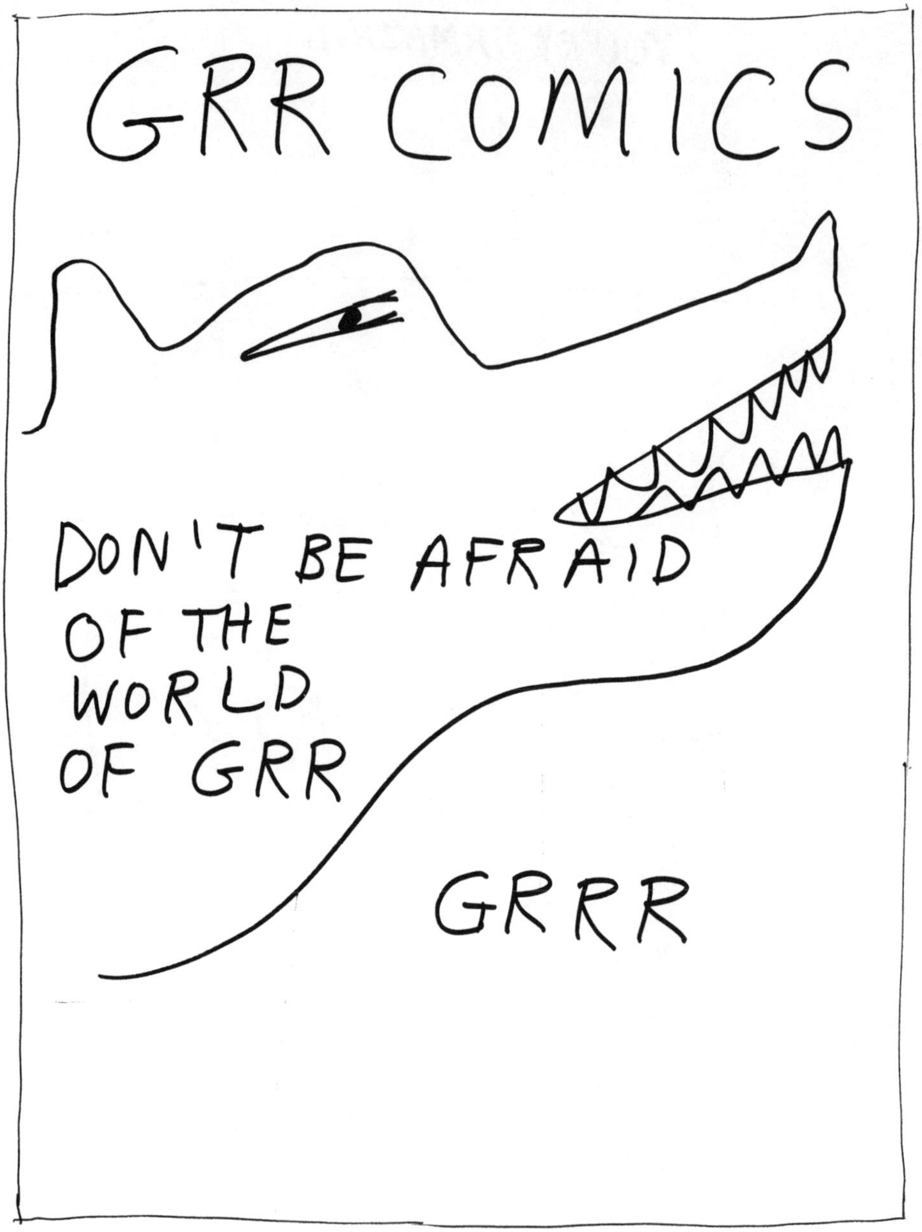
GRR COMICS
DON'T BE AFRAID OF THE WORLD OF GRR
GRRR

LEDA AND THE DOG

♪♫ AMBULATING DOWN THE STREET

WHOM SHOULD LOVELY LEDA MEET

BUT ANTON CHEKHOV

AND HIS DOG

BESIDE WHAT WOOD OR STREAM/DID

NATURE FASHION IT? LEDA ASKED THE DOG

CHEKHOV NODDED/O

BEAUTY! THE DOG BARKED/SAID.

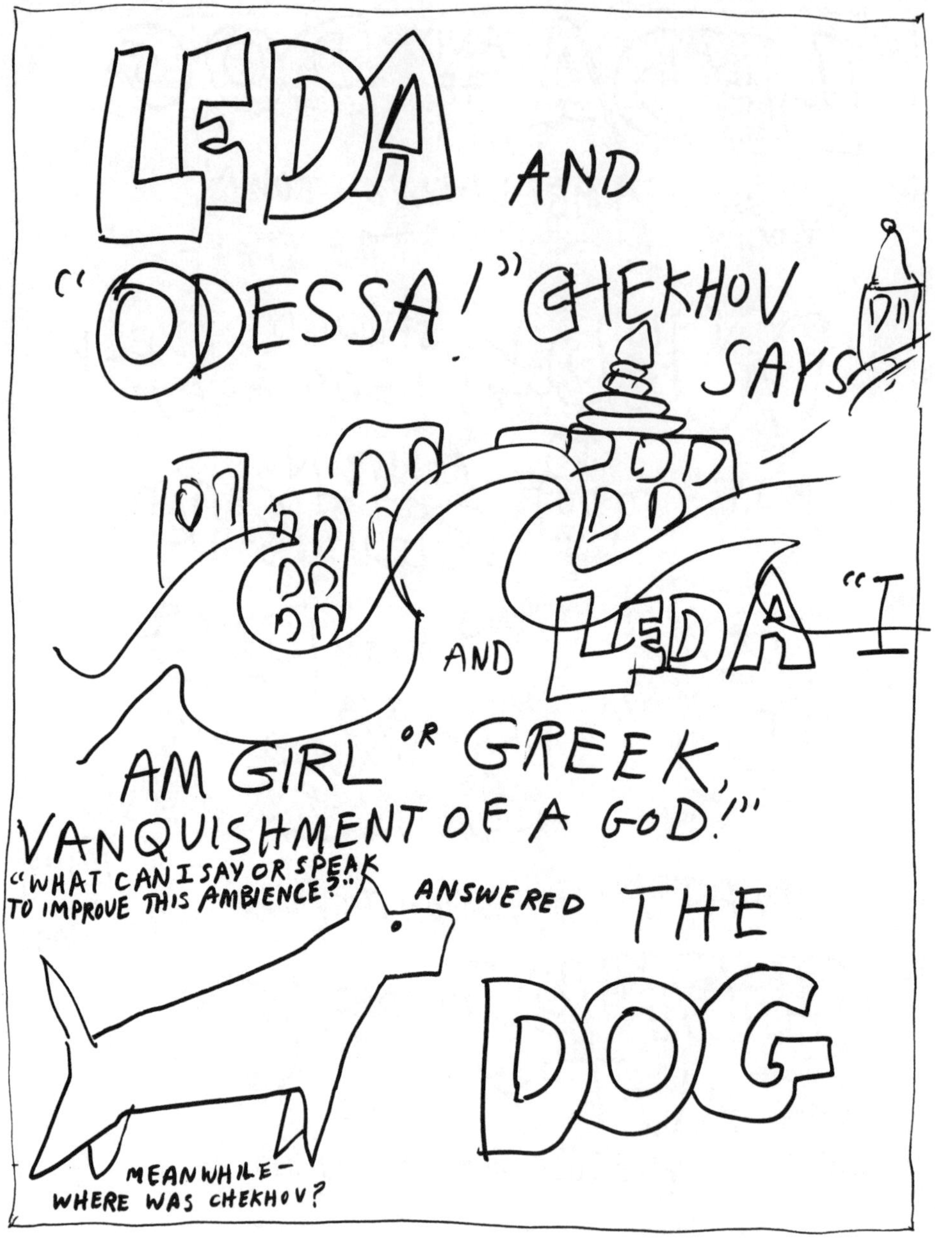
LEDA AND
"ODESSA!" CHEKHOV SAYS
AND LEDA "I AM GIRL OR GREEK, VANQUISHMENT OF A GOD!"
"WHAT CAN I SAY OR SPEAK TO IMPROVE THIS AMBIENCE?" ANSWERED THE DOG
MEANWHILE-
WHERE WAS CHEKHOV?

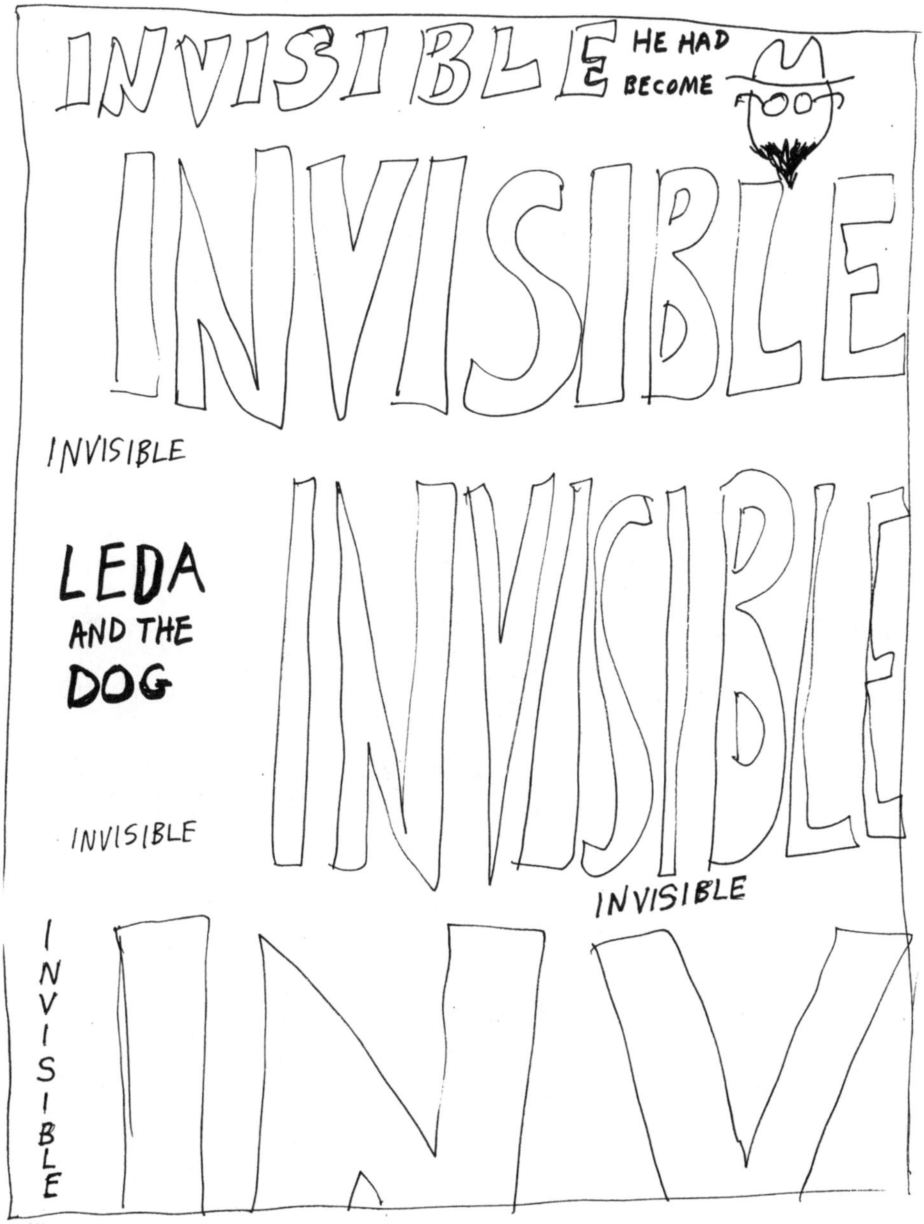
INVISIBLE
HE HAD BECOME
INVISIBLE
INVISIBLE
INVISIBLE
LEDA AND THE DOG
INVISIBLE
INVISIBLE
INVISIBLE
INV

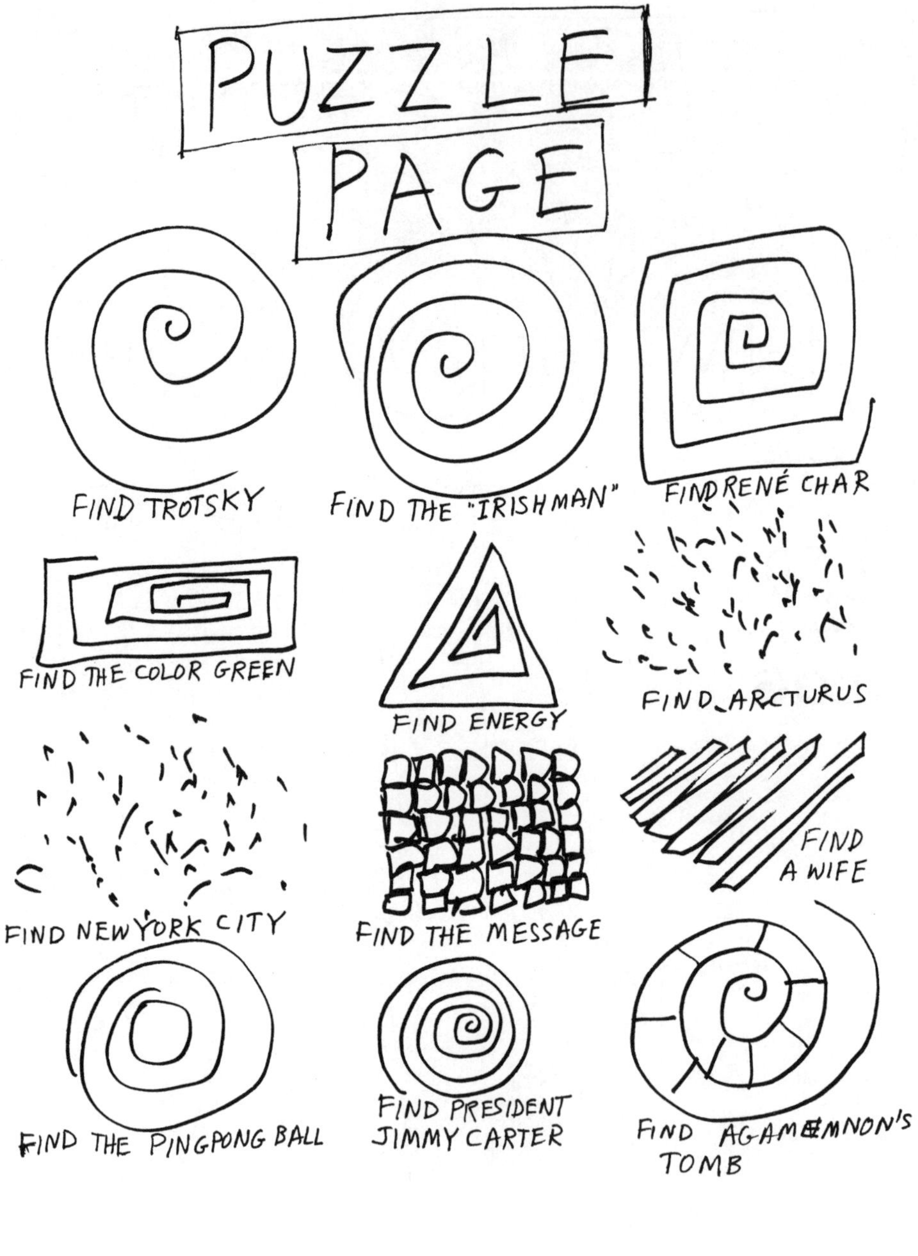
PUZZLE PAGE
FIND TROTSKY
FIND THE "IRISHMAN"
FIND RENÉ CHAR
FIND THE COLOR GREEN
FIND ENERGY
FIND ARCTURUS
FIND NEW YORK CITY
FIND THE MESSAGE
FIND A WIFE
FIND THE PINGPONG BALL
FIND PRESIDENT JIMMY CARTER
FIND AGAMEMNON'S TOMB

DEKOONING COMICS

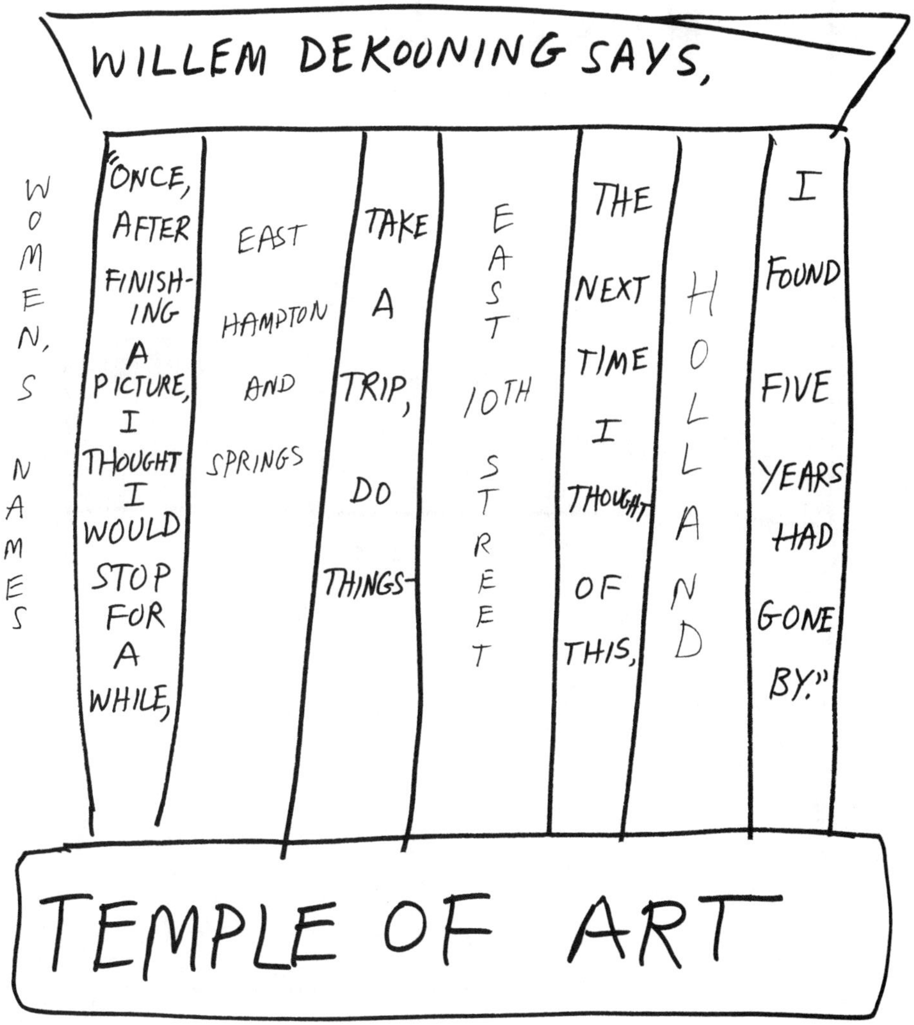
WILLEM DEKOONING SAYS,
WOMEN,S NAMES
"ONCE, AFTER FINISH-ING A PICTURE, I THOUGHT I WOULD STOP FOR A WHILE,
EAST HAMPTON AND SPRINGS
TAKE A TRIP, DO THINGS-
EAST 10TH STREET
THE NEXT TIME I THOUGHT OF THIS,
HOLLAND
I FOUND FIVE YEARS HAD GONE BY."
TEMPLE OF ART

RENNAISSANCE COMICS

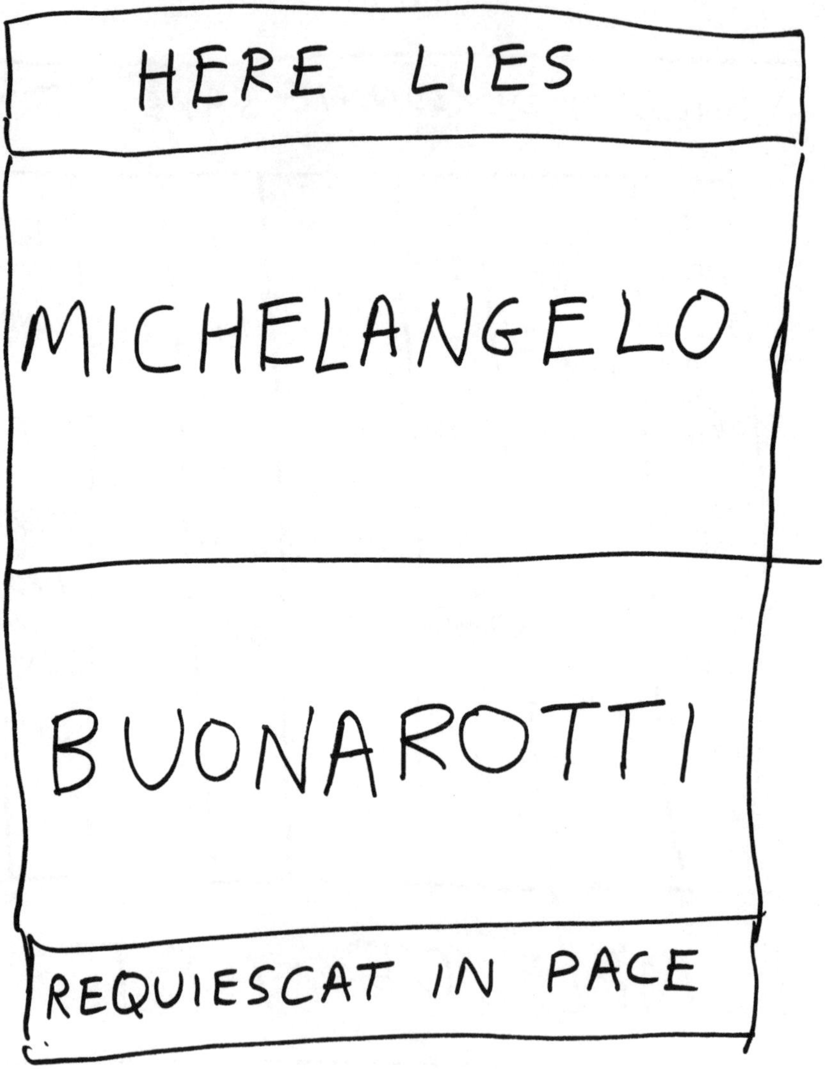
HERE LIES
MICHELANGELO
BUONAROTTI
REQUIESCAT IN PACE

PAUL KLEE COMICS

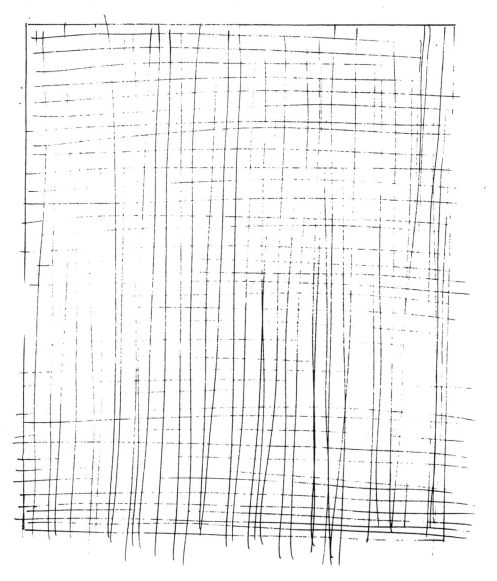

THE ARTIST IN HIS STUDIO

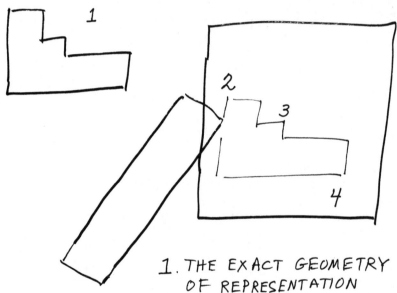

1. THE EXACT GEOMETRY OF REPRESENTATION
2. THE ARTIST FAILS TO REGULATE HIS LINES
3. PROPORTIONS BECOME INEXACT
4. HIS WORK NO LONGER REPRESENTS REALITY BUT IS A REALITY OF ITS OWN
5. PEOPLE CROWD INTO THE STUDIO TO SEE HOW THIS HAPPENS

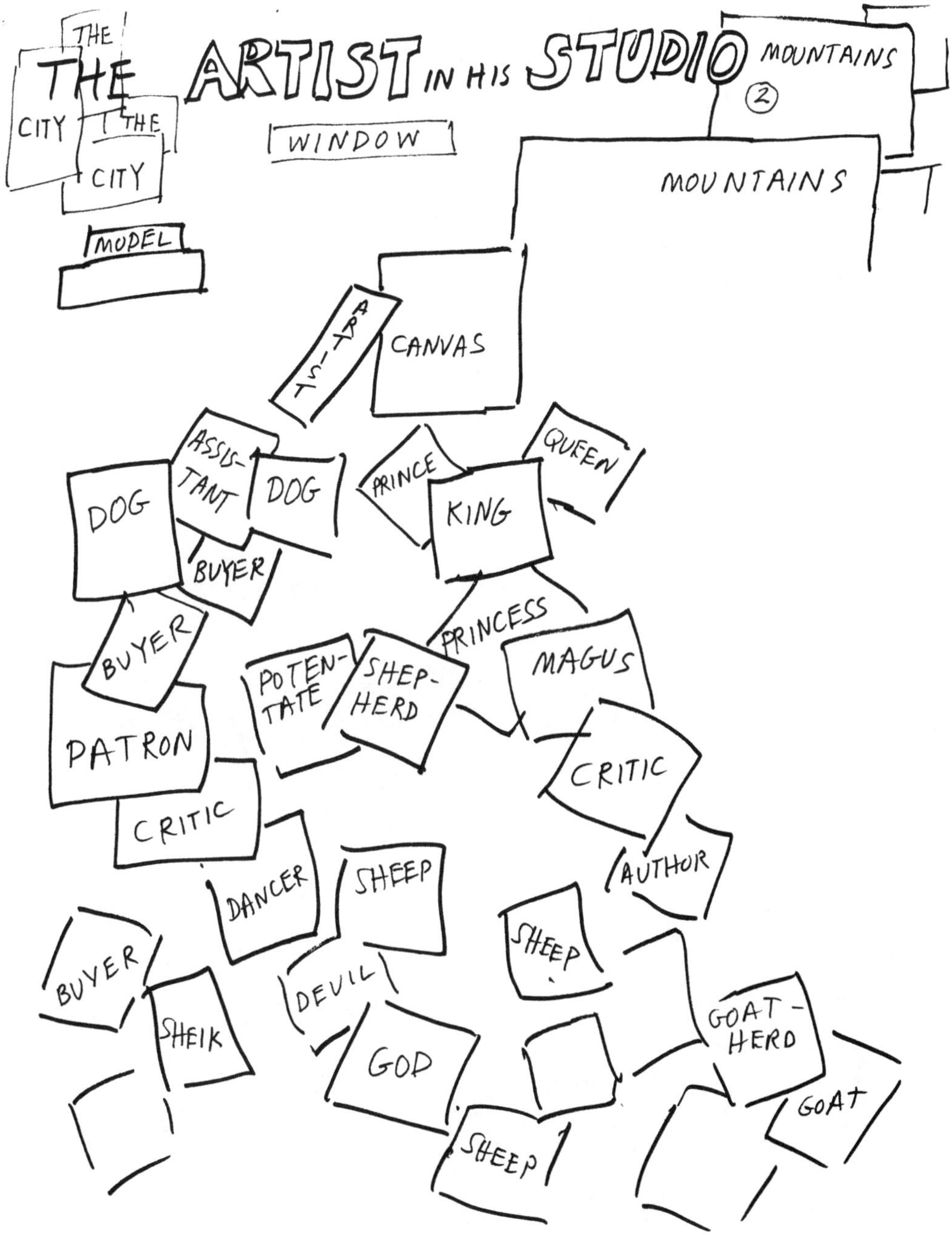
THE ARTIST IN HIS STUDIO
THE
THE
CITY
THE
CITY
WINDOW
MOUNTAINS
2
MOUNTAINS
MODEL
ARTIST
CANVAS
ASSIS-TANT
DOG
DOG
BUYER
PRINCE
KING
QUEEN
BUYER
PRINCESS
POTEN-TATE
SHEP-HERD
MAGUS
PATRON
CRITIC
CRITIC
AUTHOR
DANCER
SHEEP
SHEEP
BUYER
DEVIL
SHEIK
GOD
GOAT-HERD
GOAT
SHEEP

THE ARTIST IN HIS STUDIO
SYNTHETIC ANALYSIS

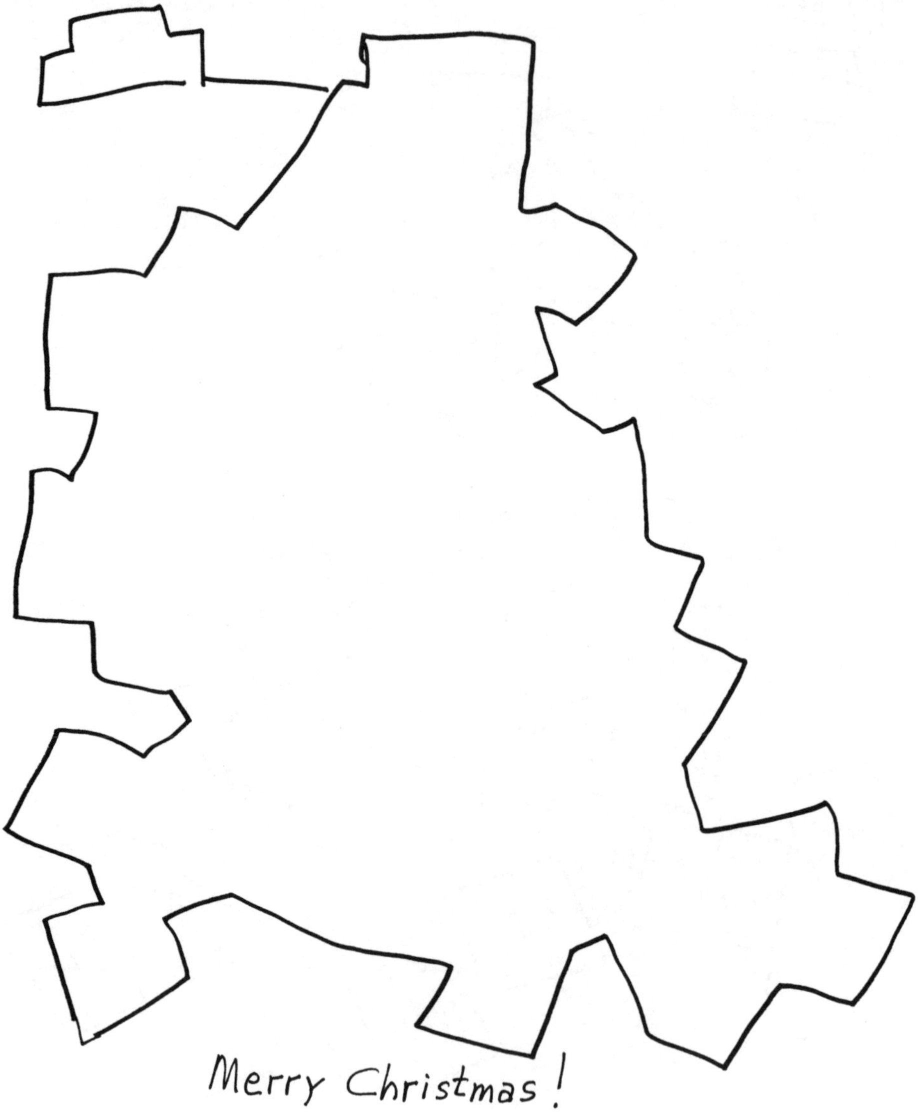

Merry Christmas!

MINNIE RADUSE

THE WILL OF ARTHUR RADUSE:

"To my niece MINEOSA (MINNIE) RADUSE I BEQUEATHE THE FIVE MILLION FREE TRAVEL MILES OWED TO ME BY AMERICAN AIRLINES AND MANY OTHER ASSOCIATED COMPANIES."

MINNIE RECEIVES THE MILES.

SHE FEELS AN URGE, EVEN A RESPONSIBILITY, TO USE THEM ALL. FIRST, SHE TRAVELS TO EGYPT.

SCARCELY HAS MINNIE ARRIVED (IN LUXOR), HOWEVER, WHEN SHE IS WHIRLED AWAY BY A SAND STORM AND CRASHED TO HER DEATH. HOWEVER,

THIS INTERESTING YOUNG BEAUTY IS SPOTTED (AND PITIED) BY THE COW-HEADED GODDESS HATHOR, WHO LEADS HER TO THE EDGE OF A SACRED RIVER (IT IS THE NILE) ON WHICH THERE IS A NARROW BOAT IN SOME WAYS LIKE A COFFIN. "COME,

MY LITTLE ONE," HATHOR SAYS. AND SHE LAYS MINNIE RADUSE DOWN IN THE BOAT AND IT IS ROWED ACROSS THE NILE TO THE "VALLEY OF THE KINGS," WHICH IS ALSO CALLED THE "LAND OF THE DEAD."

MINNIE'S MILLIONS OF FREE TRAVEL MILES LIE USELESS IN HER PURSE AS SHE MAKES THIS LONG AND SERIOUS JOURNEY FROM WHICH SHE WILL NEVER RETURN.

MINNIE RADUSE 2

MR. RAZENHAUSER, the executor of Arthur Raduse's will, BECOMES INCREASINGLY AND UNNERVINGLY AWARE THAT THERE HAS RECENTLY COME TO BE AN ENORMOUS DISPARITY IN THE AVAILABLE AND USABLE NUMBER OF FREE TRAVEL MILES, ON ALL AIRLINES.

CAN THERE BE SOME SORT OF CURSE?

HE OF COURSE THINKS OF MINNIE, WHO HAS MORE FREE MILES THAN ANY OTHER LIVING PERSON.

BUT IS SHE STILL LIVING?

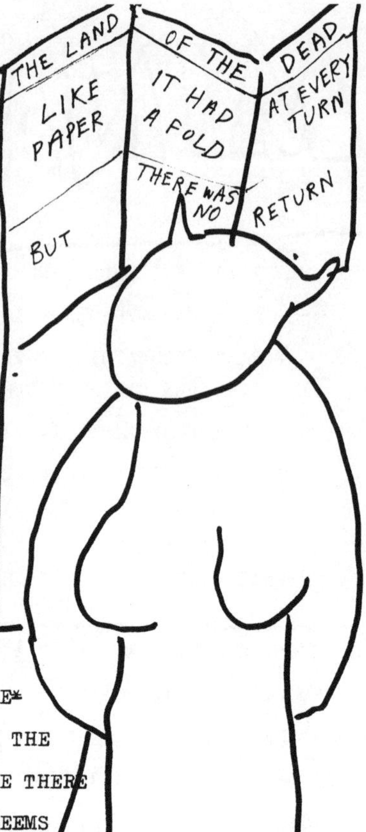
THE LAND
OF THE
DEAD
LIKE PAPER
IT HAD A FOLD
AT EVERY TURN
BUT
THERE WAS NO
RETURN

RAZENHAUSER TRAVELS TO EGYPT AND IS STRUCK BY SOMETHING HE BELIEVES HE SEES IN THE FACIAL EXPRESSION OF THE HATHOR STATUE THERE IN LUXOR. THE COW, GODDESS'S FACE SEEMS TO BE WISHING TO TELL HIM SOMETHING, BUT HE DOESN'T KNOW WHAT. (AND WHY, HE WONDERS, IN ANY CASE, WOULD SUCH A DIVINE BEING BE INTERESTED IN THE TRAVEL MILES SITUATION? RAZENHAUSER IS PUZZLED, GOES BACK TO HIS HOTEL TO SLEEP, AND FINDS A **SCARAB** IN HIS BED!

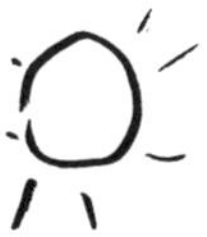

MINNIE RADUSE 3

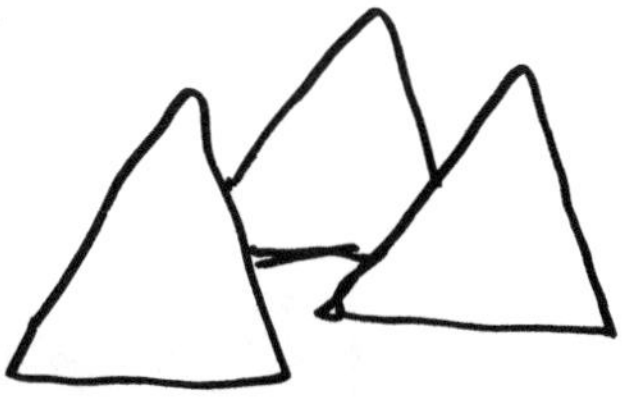

INSIDE THE SCARAB THERE ARE THREE THINGS: FIRST, THERE IS A NOTE:

Hear ye, hear ye, etc. Minnie is doing fine in the Land of the Dead. She is progressing. But these worldly travel miles could hold her back. I pray you to take them and use them someplace else. They can serve no function amongst us.

SIGNED: Hathor, Goddess of the chase, of death, of love, of child-birth, and of all other things.

SECOND, THERE ARE CHITS

FOR ALMOST FIVE MILLION

FREE TRAVEL MILES.

THIRD, THERE IS A SORT OF PIN--WITH WHICH MR. RAZENHAUSER ACCIDENTALLY SCRATCHES HIMSELF. SOON, IF HATHOR FAVORS HIM, HE WILL JOIN MINNIE AND THE KINGS.

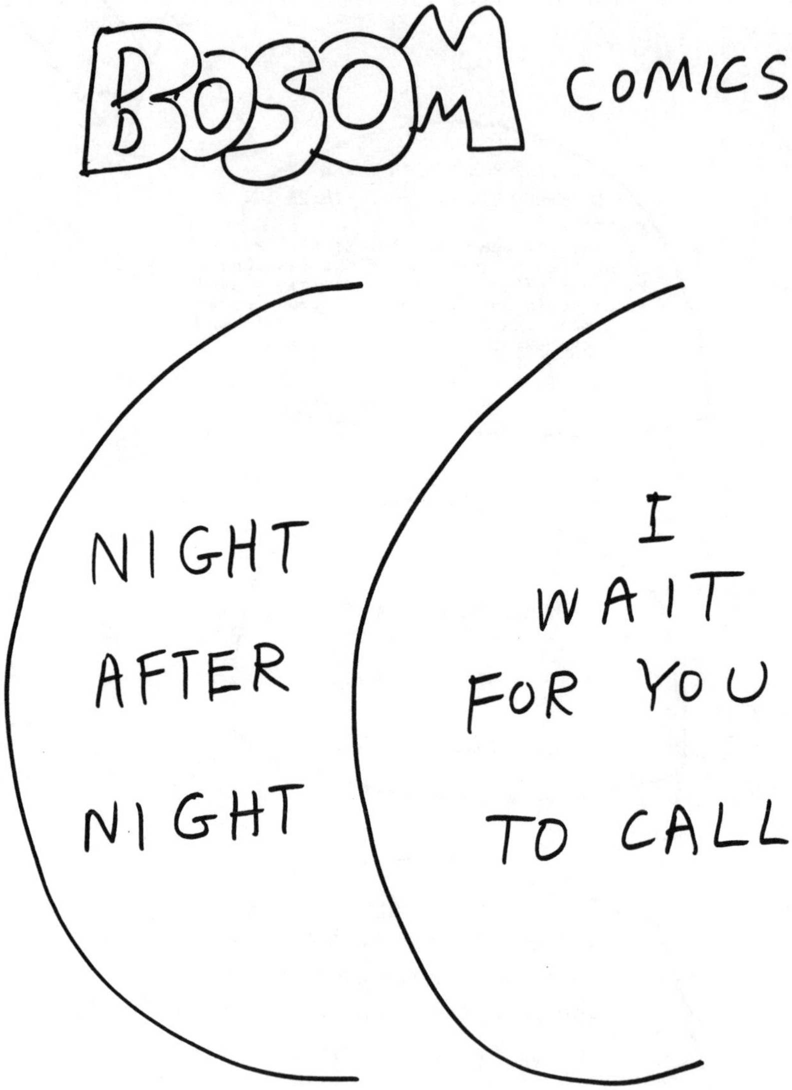
BOSOM COMICS
NIGHT AFTER NIGHT
I WAIT FOR YOU TO CALL

THE **ITALIAN** CABDRIVER COMICS

→ SAID "POETRY? POETRY

IN ENGLISH?	NAY, NAY, SIGNORE!	POETRY, POETRY	IS IN ITALIAN!
WHAT IS YOUR WORD FOR NATURE, FOR EXAMPLE?"	"NATURE," I WEAKLY SAID, KNOWING I WAS DEFEATED.	AH HAH! EXCLAIMED	MY DRIVER, LUIGI L. PICCIONE, HAILING FROM PAESTUM, LUCANIA,
BUT NOW RESIDENT IN ROME,	"IN OUR LANGUAGE—	IN OUR LANGUAGE," HE SAID,	"IT IS
LA NATURA!	IS THERE		ANY COMPARISON?"

SAD ABOUT YOU

THE PAST	GOOD DAY	BAD DAY	GOOD DAY
BAD DAY	GOOD DAY	GOOD DAY	GOOD DAY
GOOD DAY	BAD DAY	BAD DAY	BAD DAY
THE PRESENT	BAD DAY	BAD DAY	BAD DAY
BAD DAY	BAD DAY	BAD DAY	BAD DAY
DEATH	IS NOT THE WORST	OF ALL	SORROWS

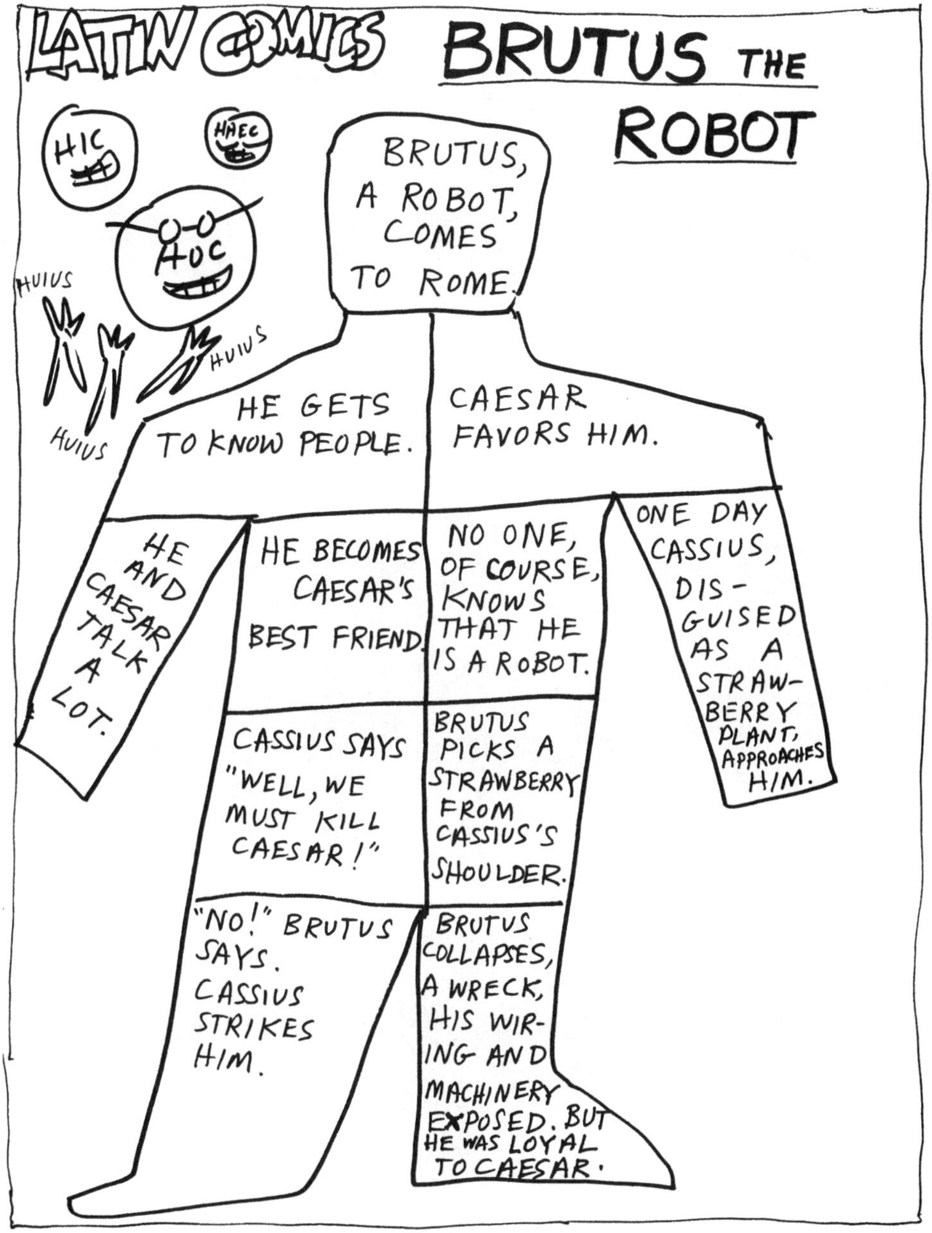

LATIN COMICS
BRUTUS THE ROBOT
HIC
HAEC
HOC
HUIUS
HUIUS
HUIUS
BRUTUS, A ROBOT, COMES TO ROME.
HE GETS TO KNOW PEOPLE.
CAESAR FAVORS HIM.
HE AND CAESAR TALK A LOT.
HE BECOMES CAESAR'S BEST FRIEND.
NO ONE, OF COURSE, KNOWS THAT HE IS A ROBOT.
ONE DAY CASSIUS, DIS-GUISED AS A STRAW-BERRY PLANT, APPROACHES HIM.
CASSIUS SAYS "WELL, WE MUST KILL CAESAR!"
BRUTUS PICKS A STRAWBERRY FROM CASSIUS'S SHOULDER.
"NO!" BRUTUS SAYS. CASSIUS STRIKES HIM.
BRUTUS COLLAPSES, A WRECK, HIS WIR-ING AND MACHINERY EXPOSED. BUT HE WAS LOYAL TO CAESAR.

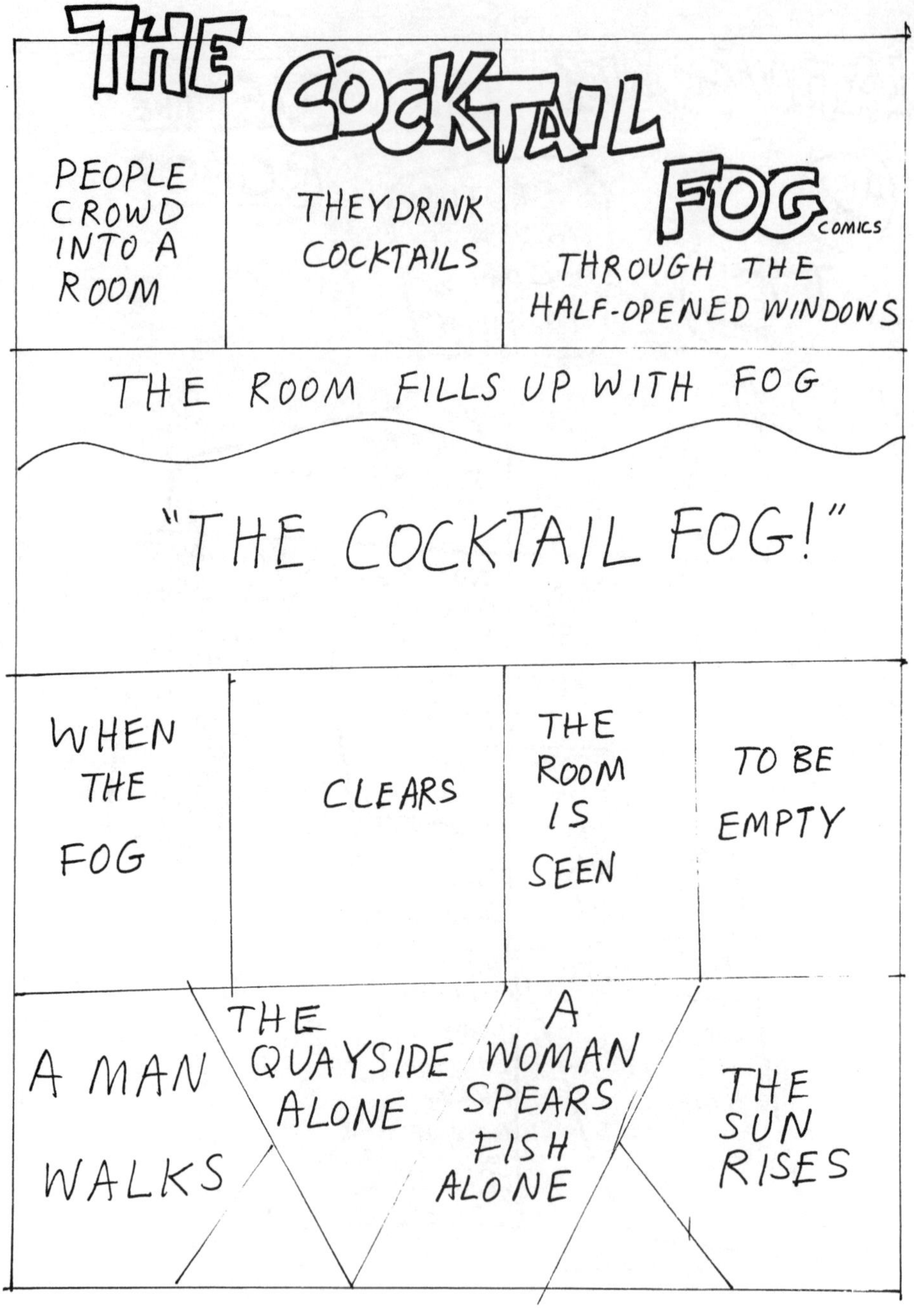
THE COCKTAIL FOG COMICS
PEOPLE CROWD INTO A ROOM
THEY DRINK COCKTAILS
THROUGH THE HALF-OPENED WINDOWS
THE ROOM FILLS UP WITH FOG
"THE COCKTAIL FOG!"
WHEN THE FOG
CLEARS
THE ROOM IS SEEN
TO BE EMPTY
A MAN WALKS
THE QUAYSIDE ALONE
A WOMAN SPEARS FISH ALONE
THE SUN RISES

OPERA HOUSE COMICS

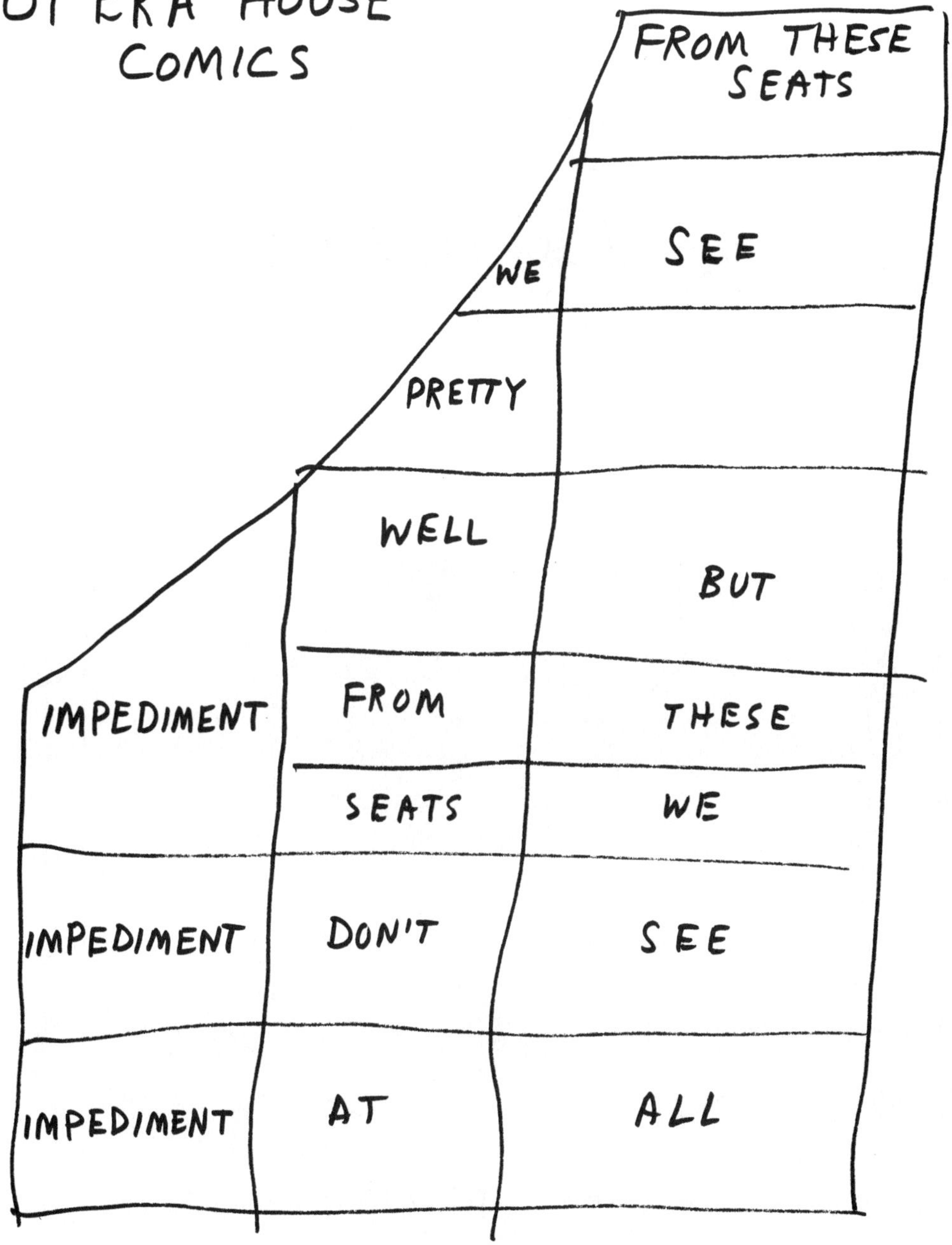
FROM THESE SEATS
WE
SEE
PRETTY
WELL
BUT
IMPEDIMENT
FROM
THESE
SEATS
WE
IMPEDIMENT
DON'T
SEE
IMPEDIMENT
AT
ALL

WHAT'S WRONG WITH THIS PICTURE?

THE MIRROR OF TIME

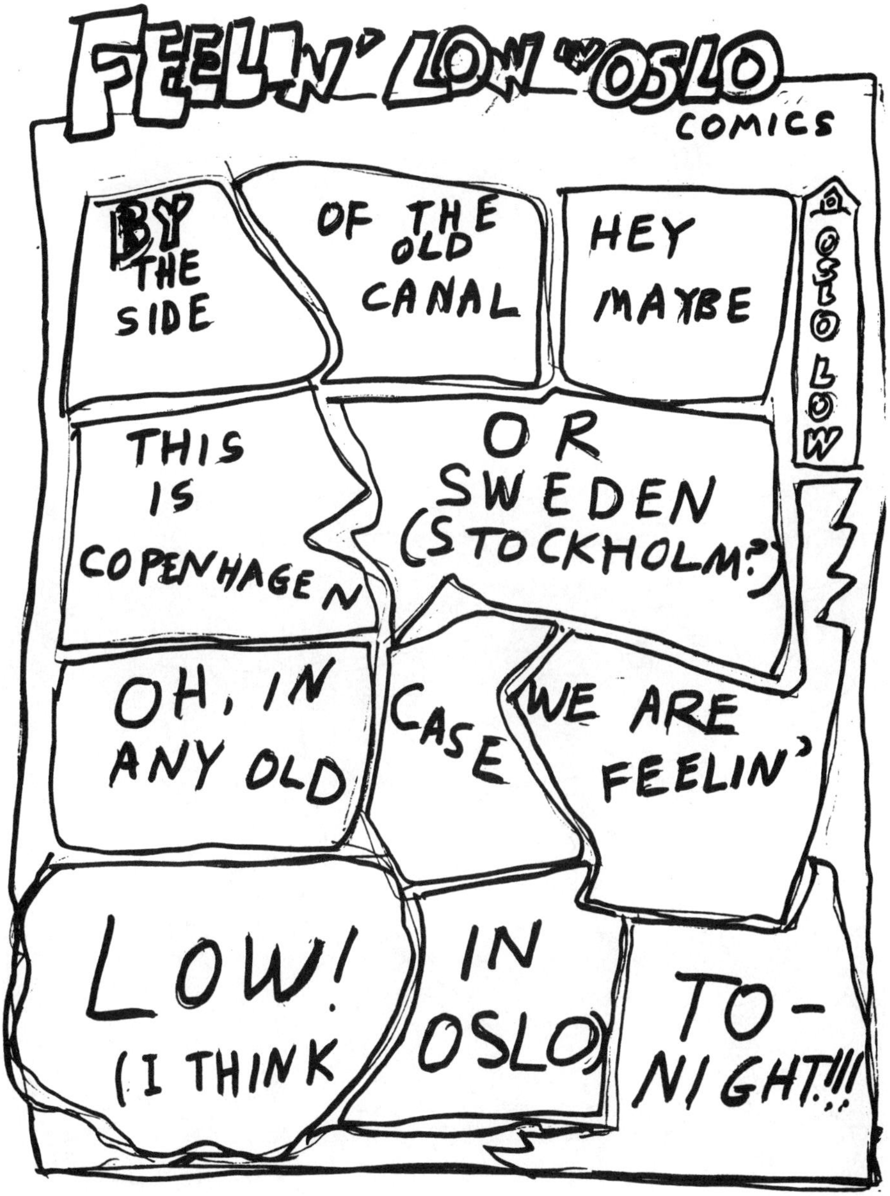
FEELIN' LOW IN OSLO
COMICS
BY THE SIDE
OF THE OLD CANAL
HEY MAYBE
OSLO LOW
THIS IS COPENHAGEN
OR SWEDEN (STOCKHOLM?)
OH, IN ANY OLD
CASE
WE ARE FEELIN'
LOW! (I THINK
IN OSLO)
TO-NIGHT!!!

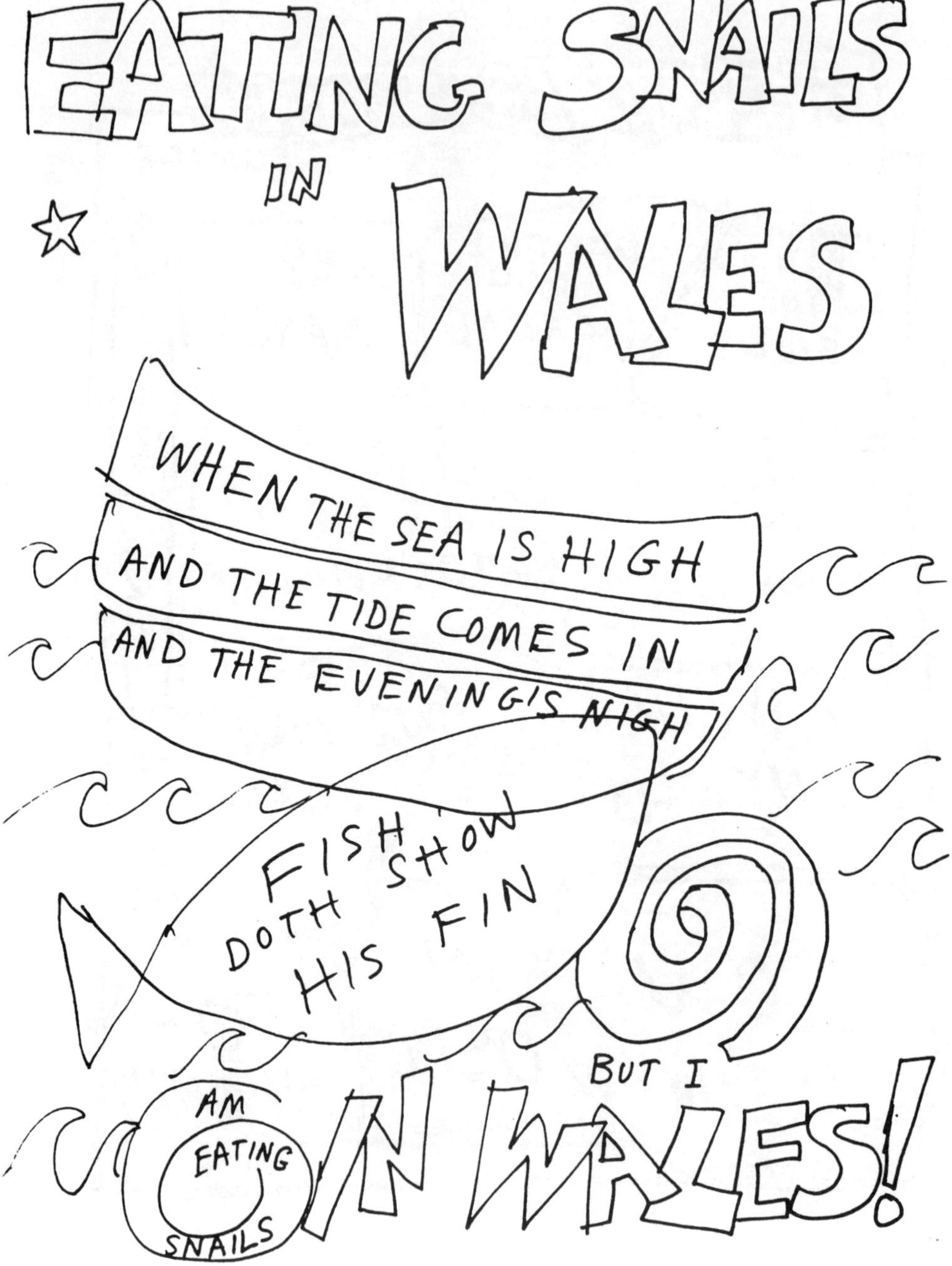
EATING SNAILS
IN
WALES
WHEN THE SEA IS HIGH
AND THE TIDE COMES IN
AND THE EVENING'S NIGH
FISH DOTH SHOW HIS FIN
BUT I
AM EATING SNAILS
IN WALES!

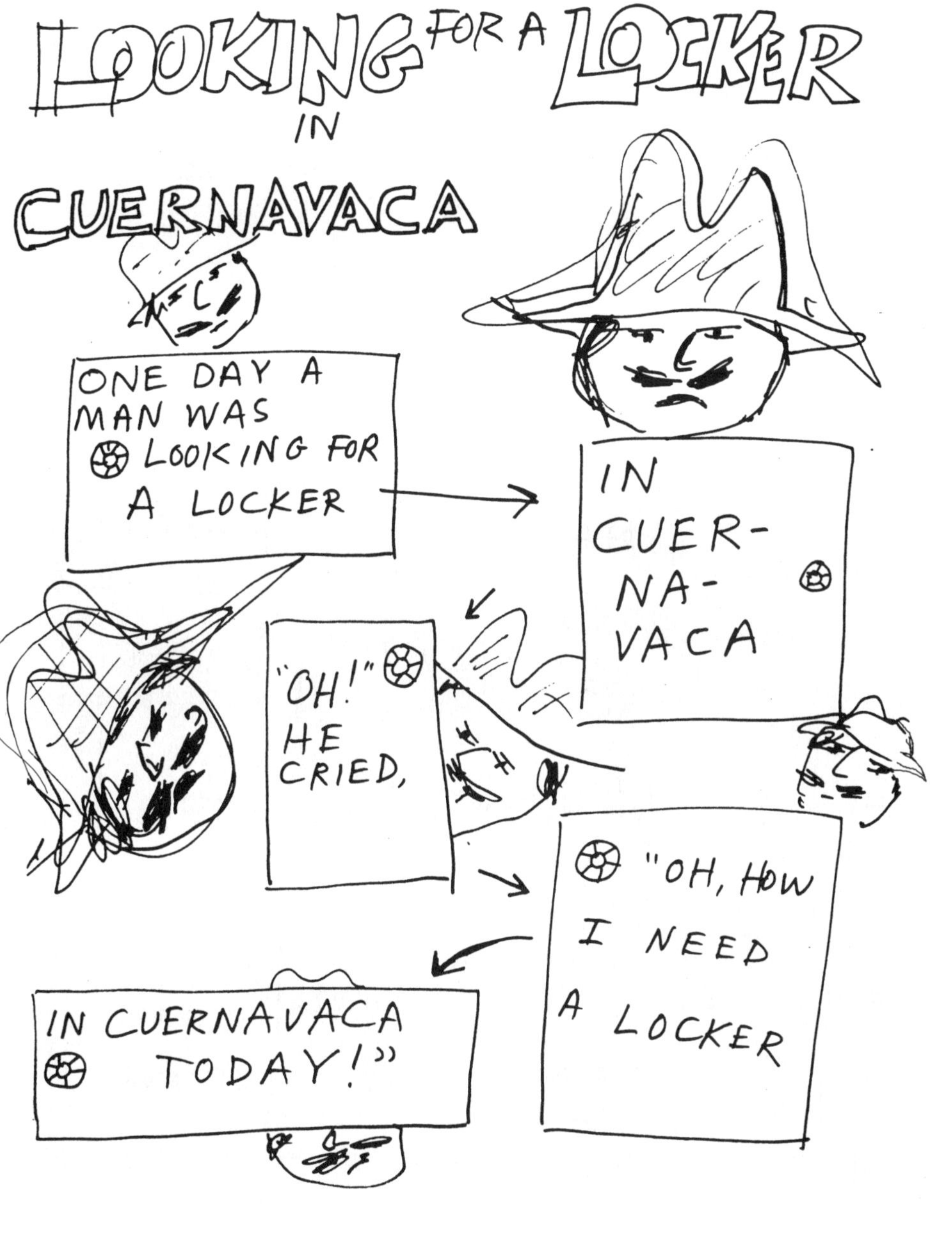
LOOKING FOR A LOCKER IN CUERNAVACA
ONE DAY A MAN WAS LOOKING FOR A LOCKER
IN CUER-NA-VACA
"OH!" HE CRIED,
"OH, HOW I NEED A LOCKER
IN CUERNAVACA TODAY!"

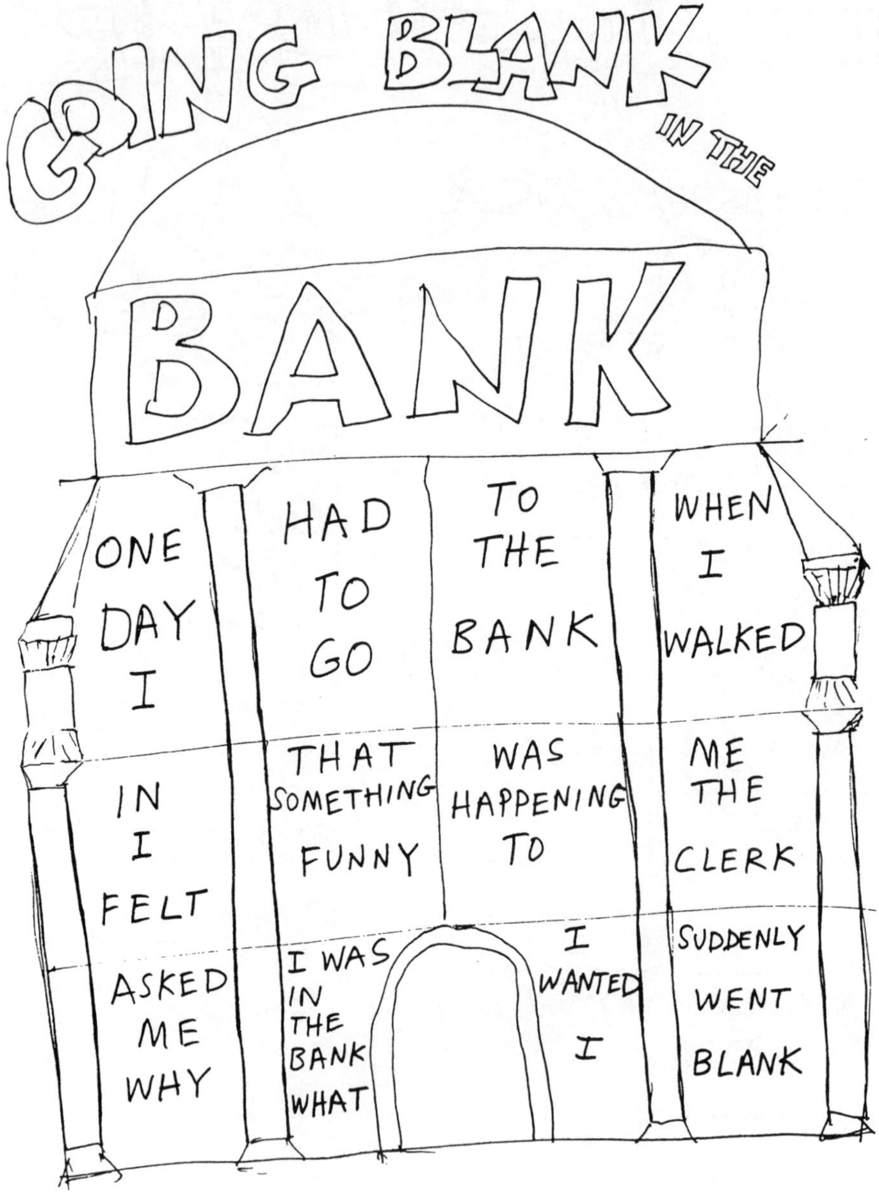
GOING BLANK IN THE
BANK
ONE DAY I
HAD TO GO
TO THE BANK
WHEN I WALKED
IN I FELT
THAT SOMETHING FUNNY
WAS HAPPENING TO
ME THE CLERK
ASKED ME WHY
I WAS IN THE BANK WHAT
I WANTED I
SUDDENLY WENT BLANK

STOPPING OFF FOR PASTRY IN ATLANTIC CITY

| HEY! | YEAH? | CAN WE GET SOME PASTRY? | WHY, SURE! |

STOPPING OFF FOR HAM IN ATLANTA

| WANT → ATLANTA → | SOME HAM? | NO | THANKS! |

STOPPING OFF FOR OUZO IN ATHENS OHIO

SHOULD WE GET SOME OUZO?

THIS IS ATHENS OHIO, NOT ATHENS GREECE!

OH

SHIT!

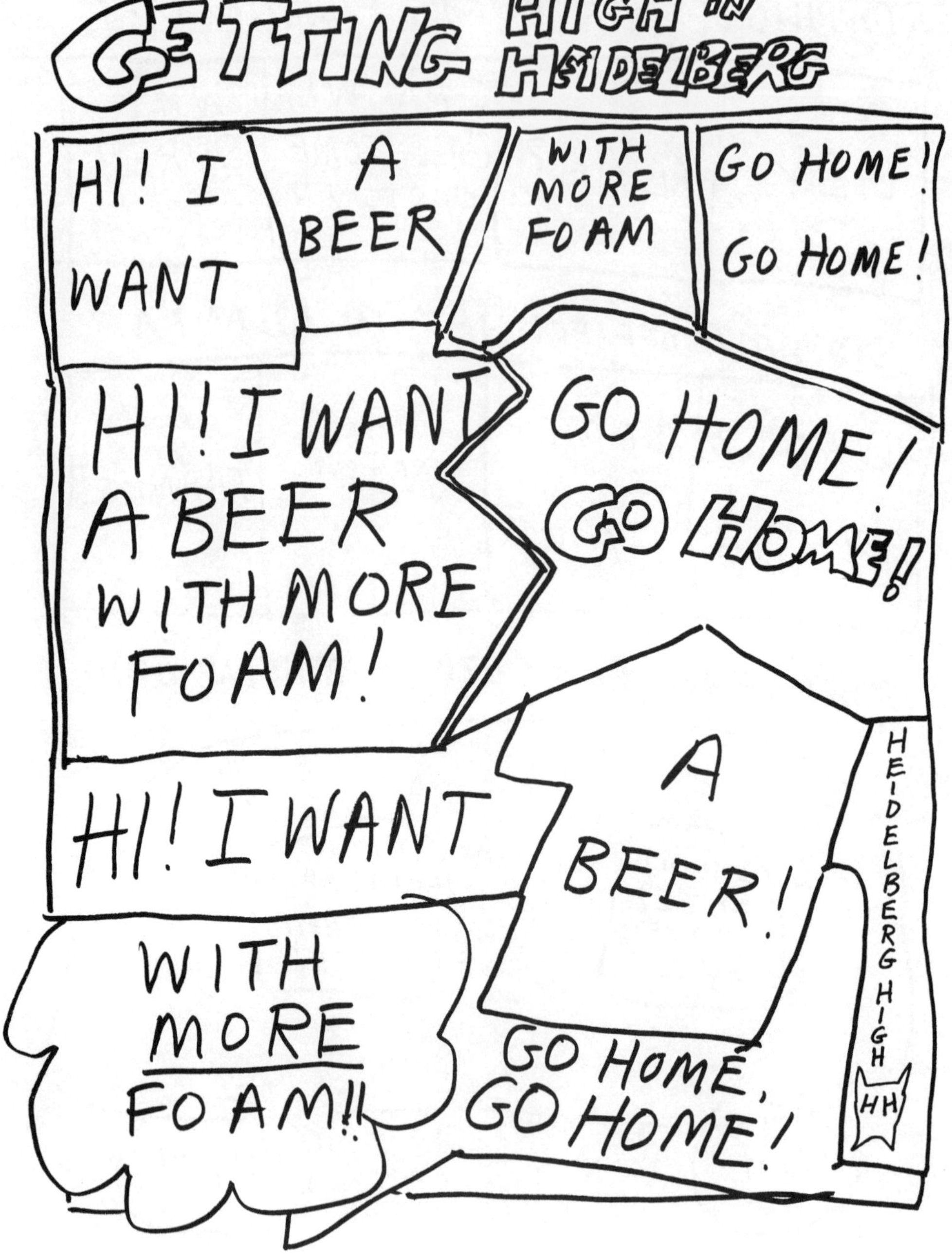
GETTING HIGH ON HEIDELBERG
HI! I WANT
A BEER
WITH MORE FOAM
GO HOME! GO HOME!
HI! I WANT A BEER WITH MORE FOAM!
GO HOME! GO HOME!
HI! I WANT
A BEER!
WITH MORE FOAM!!
GO HOME, GO HOME!
HEIDELBERG HIGH
HH

GLOBAL CHARMING
COMICS

A PHENOMENON IS ISOLATED CALLED "GLOBAL CHARMING"

HERE'S WHAT IT MEANS: EVERY DAY IN EVERY . WAY

LIFE ON EARTH BECOMES MORE AND MORE DELIGHTFUL

NONE THE-LESS, IF IT IS A FACT, IT IS A FACT

THIS IS HARD TO BELIEVE

TO BE CONTINUED...

THE END

THE PUBLISHER WISHES TO THANK. . .

SHANNA COMPTON

JORDAN DAVIS

JENNIFER GIESEKING

KAREN KOCH

AND

DAVID LEHMAN

FOR HELPING US BRING KENNETH KOCH'S MANUSCRIPT TO PUBLICATION.

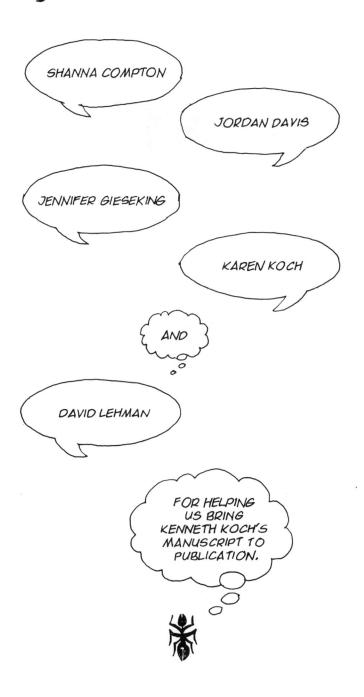

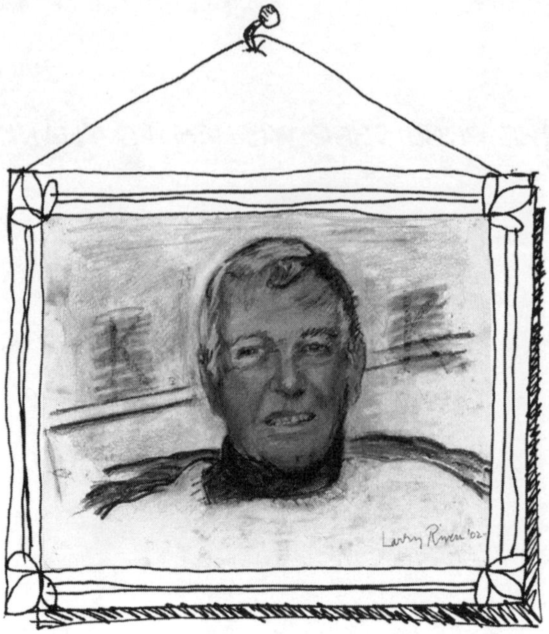
Larry Rivers '02

©LARRY RIVERS, 2002

KENNETH KOCH published many volumes of poetry, including *A Possible World*, and *Sun Out: Selected Poems 1952-1954*, both published in 2002. He was awarded the Bollingen Prize for Poetry in 1995, in 1996 he received the Rebekah Johnson Bobbit National Prize for Poetry awarded by the Library of Congress, and he received the first Phi Beta Kappa Poetry Award in 2001. Koch's short plays, many of them produced off- and off-off-Broadway, are collected in *The Gold Standard: A Book of Plays*. He also wrote several books about poetry, including *Wishers, Lies, and Dreams; Rose, Where Did You Get That Red*; and *Making Your Own Days: The Pleasures of Reading and Writing Poetry*. He taught undergraduates at Columbia University for many years. Koch died in 2002.